The Long Walk at San Francisco State *and other essays*

The Long Walk at San Francisco State

and other essays

by KAY BOYLE

GROVE PRESS, INC., NEW YORK

Portions of The Long Walk at San Francisco State *originally appeared in* Evergreen Review, *No. 76, March 1970.* Notes on Jury Selection in the Huey P. Newton Trial *originally appeared in* The Progressive, *October 1968;* No One Can Be All Things to All People *originally appeared in* Evergeen Review, *No. 81, August 1970; and* Seeing the Sights in San Francisco *originally appeared in* The Progressive, *December 1967.*

for Ira Morris

CONTENTS

The Long Walk at San Francisco State   *1*

A Listing of the Strike Demands   *68*

*The Master Plan for Higher Education
    in the State of California*   *74*

The Tactical Squad   *92*

Notes on Jury Selection
    in the Huey P. Newton Trial   *97*

No One Can Be All Things to All People   *123*

Seeing the Sights in San Francisco   *139*

The
Long
Walk
at
San
Francisco
State

I

AT A WRITER'S CONFERENCE, WHERE I WAS A MEMBER of the teaching staff, I was taken to task by the director for sitting on the grass and talking with students. The edict that the staff keep its distance from the "customers" was not written into my contract, but still it was firmly there.

On another occasion, I was not asked back by the hiring, firing, and retention committee of a university in Delaware where I had taught a summer course. This was reportedly because the closest friends I had made in the little university town were a black building contractor and his wife. George Wilson, the contractor, was putting up integrated housing, or trying to. That was ten or twelve years ago, and he was a great man then, and he will always be a great man. "There ain't no whitey in my woodpile," he would say with an explosion of laughter. In restaurants he would ask for the dark meat of chicken, saying he had trouble digesting the white. He was the first black man to walk into the Howard Johnson restaurant just outside Dover after the Finance Minister of Ghana had been refused service there. George Wilson didn't know what was going to happen, and he is too robust in spirit to seek the martyr bit. But he knew this had to be done. And they served him. "They didn't even put a screen around me," he said.

In other years, I might have done a fiction piece about that, or about the clergyman who undertook to rewrite the parables of Jesus so as to make them understandable to America's delinquent youth. But now I can only mention these things quickly in passing because of the other things that cannot wait to be said. After studying the "thought patterns" of the untamable youths he was involved with, the clergyman took the parable of the ninety and nine from the King James version of Matthew (XVIII, xii), and made it "relevant." This parable goes:

> If a man have a hundred sheep, and one of them be gone astray, doth he not leave the ninety and nine, and goeth into the mountains, and seeketh that which is gone astray? And if so be that he find it, verily I say unto you, he rejoiceth more of that sheep, than of the ninety and nine which went not astray.

The clergyman's version of this parable went:

> There was a used car lot at the corner. The owner had a hundred "heaps" on it. If one of

the "heaps" was snitched, would the owner go and look for it? You bet he would. He would never give up looking till he found it.

When things like this are being done to words, and to the lives of people behind the words, then action must be taken. A piece of writing is an act, and if I cannot manage a short story on all these strange facts, there are at least a few sentences that I can set quickly down. There is time to say that walking alone in Cambridge, Massachusetts, only a few months ago, I stopped in a darkened street and looked at the place where Harvard Law School dormitories had stood last year. A four-tier parking facility is now being constructed there, and as I stood on the corner and looked at the skeleton of girders against the night sky, I remembered that migratory birds are said to navigate their long seasonal flights by observing the stars. Men who have studied these unchanging things say that birds have memorized for their own use this small section of the celestial almanac. And I remembered something else: in those Law School dormitories that have been reduced to dust, a boy I never knew once killed himself. It was after the Christmas break, and in the note he left behind he said he was the first Harvard student in his family to have received failing grades. He said his mother had cried over this all during the holidays. There is not time to set this down in fictional terms. A novel takes at least two years to write, and the young can't wait that long to have the story of their lives and deaths

5

dredged out of the ruins. The protest must be made in other terms and as quickly as one can.

II

One night in May 1968, when I was having dinner in the home of a colleague from the English Department of San Francisco State, he received an urgent telephone call to go to the college. It was after nine, but other teachers were there, attempting to get to the Vice-President for Academic Affairs in the hope of dissuading him from inviting the police on campus. Several hundred students were sitting in the main entrance of the Administration Building, the sit-in being the culmination of a week-long crisis that had erupted between Dr. Summerskill's resignation as President and Dr. Smith's appointment to the post. "I'm going up at once," my colleague said when he came back to the table, and I said I was going with him. "Look, it's going to rain," he said—as if this would keep me from climbing Mont Blanc or crossing the Rubicon. "It's my college as much as yours," I said, which was not entirely true. He had been there several years longer, and indeed it was he who had hired me in 1963. But he finally took me along.

All the way up Nineteenth Avenue I kept asking myself what I was doing feeling committed to a college. I had lived on mountain tops, carried my babies in a rucksack on my back when I skied, believed in poets more than any other men, honored

French Resistance fighters and Italian partisans, crossed into Spain with letters from the exiled to the brave and the defiant and the imprisoned there, and brought their illicit messages out. And now, through force of circumstance, I was, of all unlikely and unsuitable things, a college professor. I was a professor, moreover, who spoke of her institution as if it were a possession of the heart. "That's because of the students," I said to myself. "That's because they're the great and vital thing."

But that wasn't entirely true either. There were other things that made State all it was. One of them was that down the hall of the Administration Building that night came Alberto Moravia, just in from Italy, choosing to arrive when one of the great social dramas of our time was being played. We had met in Rome in the last months of World War II when Moravia had come down from the mountains to his liberated city. That we should both have been at San Francisco State that night seemed to affirm that the dissension then under way was a continuation of something that had begun a long time before, a process we had both borne witness to in another time and place, and had taken our part in as well.

Moravia was bemused by the mildness of the students' demands, which were that Air Force ROTC be removed from the campus, that several hundred disadvantaged black and Third World students be admitted to the college in the Fall 1968 term, and that faculty with the same ethnic background as the students be hired to teach special courses. Young men and women all over the world were asking for far more, and asking it with greater fervor; and twenty-five years earlier Moravia had seen Italian partisans ask for an entire country, an entire people, and get a good portion of what they asked. He showed a bleak interest in the report that a troika composed of the Vice-President for Academic Affairs, the Vice-President for Business Affairs, and the Dean of Students had been locked in an office that afternoon by the students. Once liberated, the three men were in no frame of mind to listen to faculty recommendations that they walk down the hall and discuss the students' grievances. The teachers who urged this solution were certain that if the students had been asked to go home and send a delegation the following day, they would have cheered. A monsoon-like rain was beating down outside, and although they sang that they would not be moved and that they would overcome, it had been a long week, and many of them were stupefied by lack of sleep, and their spirits were low.

Just before the first police units appeared, Moravia was whisked away by friends, for this was no place for a citizen of another country. And as four uniformed keepers of the peace advanced down the long empty hall to the scene of weariness and disjointed song, I walked toward them, feeling in that moment solitary and unfettered, as every individual alive has the right to feel at every instant of his life. When we had come face to face, I said to the four men: "Gentlemen, you may go no farther. This campus belongs to the faculty and students, not to the police." The sergeant, a short, undistinguished man who carried a walkie-talkie that crackled with messages directly from God, barely glanced at me as he said, "Aw, lady, come off it"; and the four of them marched directly through me, as if I had as little substance as a cloud.

I could have pursued them and pounded my fists against their dark blue backs as they made for the closed door of the troika authority. Or I could have stopped them short by telling them a thing I had learned at a three-day conference on suicide I had taken part in six months before. The conference had drawn attention to statistics showing the high rate of nervous breakdowns and subsequent suicides among members of police forces throughout America. There had been discussion as to whether the pressure of their work had brought so many to the point of taking their own lives, or if it was the particular combination of characteristics which had originally led them to choose the role that ultimately caused their self-inflicted deaths. Training in the violent punishment, and even extinction, of others, it was suggested, might bring them more readily than other men to the act of drawing their service revolvers from their holsters and, frequently standing before a mirror, blowing out their own brains instead of those of fellow citizens whose class or color they happened to dislike. I could have told the policemen about this. But I ended up doing nothing. I was on a year's probation, having served twenty-one days in Santa Rita Prison following my second arrest for sitting down in a doorway of the Oakland Induction Center, and that year was just beginning. I felt I didn't have any more time to give to that or any other interruption to the living of daily life. I did not know of the daily turmoil that lay ahead for everyone at State.

At midnight the patrol wagons began drawing up in the Holloway Avenue parking lot. Sixty persons were arrested, among them members of the American Federation of Teachers, Local 1352, who volunteered to be taken into custody in place of some of the students. What purpose these arrests served it is impossible to say. Did the police action prove the absurd futility of locking administrators in an office, or did it, on the contrary, call public and administrative attention to the students' demonstration and thus create a wider understanding of the need for an open Economic Opportunity Program? Did the subsequent prison sentences and fines serve to break the spirits of students and faculty to such an extent that they would act with greater propriety in the future? But less than six months later, students would be demonstrating in increasing numbers, and faculty would be marching in support of their demands. What I did learn that night was that there is no chance at all if you try to do it alone. One AFT member was to say later that "the record of faculty action must cease to be a record of faculty impotence." The following day I joined the AFT.

That night in May marked the moment when San Francisco State ceased to be a place that I went to for the purpose of meeting with students, either in classes or in conference. Almost without warning, it became a concerned state of mind, much as a country, particularly in defeat, sheds its actual soil and takes on a richer meaning. All that followed was a part of the sequence of engagements in an unending battle for something one might as well call decency, a battle in which the ardent and powerless have little chance to win. This began almost without warning, I have said, but at least one warning had been given me. During the previous winter I had sought to sponsor the writing course of Sonia Sanchez, the black poet who had been teaching a course for no credit in the Experimental College at State (and this in a college where you can get credit for a course in bowling). Although the engagement fought to sponsor Sonia Sanchez was eventually won, I took no pride at all in the triumph, for in the process I had lost too much pride in the potential for forthright action of those in the college administration who obstructed the way.

The ways of academic procedure, being new to me, are deeply puzzling. I can still see no reason, for instance, for the vast amount of printed matter, largely from department heads, that day after day fills our mailboxes to overflowing. These communications keep us informed of absolutely everything except the truth of how things are. At no time was I given a Xeroxed directive telling me that I, or anyone else, was not permitted to sponsor a black teacher's course in the English Department, no matter how exceptional the qualifications of that teacher, and that I'd better forget about it. That was probably the one notice they forgot to put in my box.

As of October 31, 1968, Black Panther George Murray, Minister of Information of the Panther Party, became the main (and oversimplified) issue for the media in its reporting on the growing tensions at San Francisco State. Murray was a student at the college as well as a teacher of approximately one hundred Special Admissions students. In September, the Trustees had requested President Smith to assign Murray to a non-teaching post because of his alleged advice to minority students to arm themselves for self-protection. Smith declined to do so on the grounds that Murray was entitled to due process, and pointed out that college disciplinary proceedings were already under way against Murray for his part in a violent fracas which had taken place in the office of the college newspaper, *The Daily Gater,* late in 1967. But on the last day of October 1968, Chancellor Dumke ordered Smith to suspend Murray both as student and teacher. When Smith reluctantly complied, faculty members were shocked into an awareness that their own positions at the college were probably no more secure from remote political control than Murray's, even if their skins happened to be white.

The order for Murray's suspension was not an isolated act. It was simply the most recent move in the ruthless repression of black men and women who demand to be recognized as black, who demand to be taught black history by black teachers, and who know with passion and impatience the vocabulary of the language they wish to speak, and the meaning of the degrees they wish to hold. The suspension of Murray was just one more instance of effacing one more black individual from the record of those who are permitted to function as human beings in a white society. This is a procedure that is being enforced in California both on and off campus, including the legally sanctioned murder of members of the Black Panther Party by Bay Area police. At least once every twenty-four hours I remember the words that Hannah Arendt wrote recently: "The great rarity of slave-rebellions and of uprisings among the disinherited and downtrodden is notorious; on the rare occasions when they occurred it was precisely 'mad fury' that turned dreams into nightmares for everybody, and in no case, as far as I know, was the force of mere 'volcanic' outbursts, as Sartre states, 'equal to that of the pressure put on' the oppressed." *

III

Sonia Sanchez, a tiny, child-like figure with an enormous black aureole of hair around her small, tense face, was now in the second semester of teach-

* Hannah Arendt, "Reflections on Violence," *The New York Review of Books*, February 27, 1969.

ing credit courses in the English Department at San Francisco State. I sat in on the night sessions and listened to her woo from the eight or ten black students in the class the everyday vocabulary of their lives. She asked them to set down on paper the things that were driving them nuts, and to get these things down in their own words, not in the language of some other writer whose books they had been asked to read sometime, somewhere. No white teacher had ever made them believe that the way they spoke, and what they thought, was worth writing about. All they had ever learned in other classrooms was what a problem they were to a troubled white society.

Sonia Sanchez was putting into practice the curriculum the Black Students Union (BSU) was fighting for: an area of learning that was connected to black people's lives by a language that did not belittle or confuse them. In those night sessions her students wrote poetry that would have meaning to others in their community, and that is probably one of the things that good writing is. Like the others, I wrote poems in Sonia Sanchez's classroom, but the trees and mountains and winds and sand and sea I wrote of were scenic props. They had no more relevance to life and death than a lace handkerchief discreetly dropped into the bellowing anguish of a slaughterhouse. There were four-letter, and five-letter, and frequently twelve-letter words in the poems the students wrote and read aloud. It is quite possible none of them knew Sonia Sanchez's poem "malcolm" or her "Memorial

—To Bobby Hutton." "Malcolm" was, of course, Malcolm X, and Bobby Hutton was a seventeen-year-old Black Panther who, one spring night in 1968, in his undershorts, with his hands held high above his head, was riddled with bullets as he obeyed the order to walk to a police car. But even if they did not know her poetry, they knew that Sonia was asking them to speak and write in a college classroom a language that they had always been reluctant to write, or to speak too loud, before.

One of my students was Eduardo Guerrero, who, on the afternoon of November 13, 1968, stood in his pea jacket left over from three years in the Navy, fists full of clay and rock clawed from the excavation for a new building going up on campus. He was about to smash this mixture into the plastic-masked faces of the Tactical Squad.* Officers of the Squad had just beaten and arrested more than a dozen students and they were now waiting in formation, clubs readied, for whatever violence they could manage to incite. Eduardo's thoughts run quicker than mercury in his skull. He is black, he wears a well-shaped helmet of hair, and his bones seem as delicate and breakable as those of a young deer. But he is neither breakable nor delicate. "Be men, man!" he was shouting at the cops. "Let's see your eyes!" I dropped the sign I was carrying, and

* See page 92

there it lay in the turmoil of feet in the yellow clay, still saying as best it could: NOW IS THE TIME FOR ALL GOOD MEN TO STAND WITH US, FOR A COLLEGE FREE FROM RACISM! FOR A COLLEGE FREE FROM POLITICAL TYRANNY!

I flung my arms around Eduardo's pea jacket, and he reared like a colt when you try to get a halter on it, seeking furiously to shake me off. "Let me do my thing!" he shouted; but I know that his "thing" is made up of other considerations. It is partly telling people exactly what Melville had in mind about race relations when he wrote *Benito Cereno* ("Dig, you dig?" Eduardo asks after every sentence); it is partly describing in a term paper how mushrooms look at sunrise, and dusk growing on a hillside in Mexico; and another part is explaining what went wrong with Hemingway ("You dig?") long before Eduardo himself was born. But at this particular moment of violence I said I was going to give him an F in the course if he stepped out of his rightful role. This was my own nonviolent and authoritarian weapon, my uncondonable pulling of rank. But I know it wasn't the words I cried out—and this is my consolation—but something quite different that made him drop the clay and rocks as if they were coals burning his hands. Perhaps he remembered Dylan Thomas saying: "I agree with Schopenhauer (who, in his philosophic dust, would turn with pleasure at my agreement) that life has no pattern and no purpose, but that a twisted vein of evil, like the poison in a drinking glass, coils up from the pit to the top of the hem-locked world."

However it was, soon after that Eduardo got himself a movie camera—or was given one through one of those federal projects that have now perished for lack of funds—and he went down to Mississippi to show anyone who wanted to learn how to make films to supplement even more fully the wretched document of black American history. Eduardo is too cynical to be a good militant, for he is not even partially myopic. He sees oppression very clearly and bitterly with both eyes. But then what about my student John Lovejoy, a white man, who has never been oppressed? "Four wasted Air Force years behind you," he wrote of himself, "and now you decide to begin fighting at last those other forces that have enmeshed you for so long." How did John Lovejoy get where he is?

On that day that Eduardo Guerrero armed him-self with rocks and clay, a group of teachers, en-tirely without premeditation, marched between the students and the shatterproof, visored police in silent and shaken protest against the fury of the police attack that had taken place moments before. The Tactical Squad, supported by busloads of the regular police force, was then holding more than a thousand students at bay. It was a singular moment of triumph (and there were few enough such mo-ments) as the walkie-talkies of the Tac Squad were heard directing the men to "retreat, but slowly; retreat, but slowly," and the Squad began backing, step by measured step, to the escape hatches of the patrol vans that lined the parking lot. And as they retreated, we advanced, bearing our signs, and the massed students broke into applause. Some of the young women among them were in tears as they cried out: "Our loyal faculty has come!"

There is no satisfactory answer why, in that one solitary instance, the police retreated. Perhaps some higher order had been given that we, arms linked now as we stood between the students and the cops, had not been permitted to hear. At that moment I wanted to believe it was the sudden affirmation, before their plastic-shielded eyes, of the new alliance between teachers and students that made useless the thirty-inch batons they clutched in both hands. We were aligned against the entire immediate world, against the administration, the public, the college Trustees. We, both students and faculty, knew that the Trustee group all over the country is ninety-six percent white, seventy-five percent Protestant, eighty-six percent male, and seventy-three percent businessmen over fifty. Yet our signs called on them—in the hypocritical voices the young have had enough of—to come forward and negotiate.

That was Black Wednesday, November 13, 1968. On the following day the front-page headlines of *The Daily Gater* voiced the general outrage. COP TERRORISM ON CAMPUS! TAC SQUAD CLUBS STUDENTS! the two-inch letters cried out, while the smaller print told the senseless story:

18

. . . The cops were let loose from their stronghold in the men's gym basement boiler room because a newsman and a campus security officer had been attacked. [It was later concluded that the newsman and the campus guard had come into conflict with each other. Indeed, on that day a KGO–TV cameraman allegedly clubbed two students with his camera, knocking one unconscious.] . . . The brutality began shortly after 12:30 P.M., when Black Students Union members were returning to their office from a press conference they had been holding.* A squad of eleven blue-helmeted cops marched in two's toward the office . . . [then] at least two Tac Squad members rushed and attacked BSU leader Nesbitt Crutchfield. The officers pushed Crutchfield against the north wall . . . and hit him in the mid-section to double him over. The cops then hit Crutchfield on the back with their thirty-inch clubs and knocked him down. After Crutchfield fell, one cop kneed him in the back while the other clubbed him . . .

Patrol wagons were drawn up on Holloway Avenue, and at least a dozen students, seized at random from the massed crowd that now attacked the police with rocks, clods of earth, bottles, and pieces of wood, were arrested. Their hands were manacled behind their backs as they entered the vans, and some were bleeding profusely. I wanted to go away and witness no more of it. But too many people all

* See page 68

over the world were doing just that, and I knew I didn't have the right to go.

IV

On November 4th, the Black Students Union, after three years of broken promises on the vital issue of a Black Studies Program at State, made public its ten non-negotiable demands and announced that it would call a strike "to focus national and international attention on our situation in this college." The following day, the Third World Liberation Front (TWLF) voted to support, and participate in, the strike, and on November 7th it specified its own five demands.* These fifteen non-negotiable demands were all directed toward clearly stated and entirely reasonable goals: the implementation of a Black Studies Department and an Ethnic Studies Institute at the college, each with full departmental autonomy. The specified curricula would connect with the black and Third World economy. Black students were not for a moment asking the indulgence of a mystical experience of their black cultural past, but for the relevant knowledge of how to meet their people's educational hopes, and how to give substance to their people's desperate political needs. Black men, for instance, are largely unemployed. This is a vital factor to be taken into account in the planning of the black students' college courses, and not

* See page 69

the family structure of the white society. IQ tests are looked upon as a device that measures only the degree of familiarity with middle-class white culture.

On November 5th, Stokely Carmichael spoke on campus and urged Third World students to turn to confrontation politics in order "to heighten the contradictions within American racist institutions." But these words, and this intent, were already an integral part of the activist students' vocabulary, and they had scarcely the time to listen to him speak. On November 6th, the strike got under way, with students picketing the college buildings, entering classrooms in "education teams," and finally holding a mass rally which climaxed in a march on the Administration Building. President Smith sent out word that he was too busy to meet with students, and the disruption of classes then intensified. As black and Third World students cleared building after building, lively and valuable dialogue took place, and there were teachers who temporarily relinquished their authority to the invaders and sat down as students themselves to listen to them speak. There were also instances of scuffling as other teachers and students resisted. The white of terror in people's faces and the high wind of panic in their voices brought the Tactical Squad in without delay. Smith described the situation to newsmen as "the most acute crisis this campus has ever faced," but still no meeting with the student leaders was initiated. Throughout that campus to which he referred, there was a growing feeling that the disruptions could have been handled by the (unarmed) campus police, and the issues at least temporarily resolved had negotiations been initiated.

San Francisco State campus is almost entirely without beauty. Its buildings are contemporary, low-brow "renaissance," and unlovely, offering not a cornice, or pillar, or curved balustrade in esthetic confirmation of Man's questionable nobility. There are no architectural flights with which his soaring spirit might be induced to compete. The grassy areas are undistinguished except for a shady nave of redwood trees that leads damply from the steps of the Business and Social Science Building to— what? In lofty, mysterious sorrow, these mighty trees flank a walk that is not unlike a cathedral aisle, and every step of the way that gradually descends between the heroic redwood trunks is one more dark promise of what *has* to lie beyond. But nothing lies beyond except the malodorous college cafeteria, the Commons, squatting, glassy-eyed, without any structural past or future, on the slope below.

In warm, fair weather, students had always stretched out on the grass to talk or sleep or hold somebody's hand, often with their dogs or babies, and on those days a deceptive sense of well-being had lulled the fears of the uneasy. (For was not the towering nave of trees that finally led to nothing saying something about the situation of higher education in the State of California? Confused though the metaphor may have been, still the suggestion was persistently there.) But now every sign of the fair, warm weather was gone, and nearly three thousand students, some with their dogs and babies accompanying them still, circulated through the campus to the cadence of: "On strike! Shut it down! On strike! Shut it down!" From the moment this march began, a small group of teachers, walking separately from the chanting students, formed a vigil line in support of the students' demands. Even if there was no decisive action one could take, and even if ringing statements reached only sympathetic ears, still there was no way for the outraged to sit down in their offices or enter their classrooms with mayhem taking place outside. We would teach our students elsewhere—in temples, in churches, on the beach, in our front sitting rooms or our backyards, but not in Fortress San Francisco State. That territory was suitable for nothing now except the bearing of signs that asked the faraway Trustees not to leave the matter of the future of the college to the police but to concern themselves with a discussion of the students' "non-negotiable" demands.

My children weren't small enough any more to be carried in a rucksack on my back on that long walk we made, but there was one Chicano student who could perhaps have qualified. Whenever he had had enough of chanting with the others, he would bring himself in his striped cotton jeans and his tight little leather jacket over to the faculty line to get some information about the stars. He had black hair almost to his shoulders, straight as a piece of silk, flat, high, golden cheekbones, and a neck so breakable it seemed the sharpness of his voice might snap it in two. He was seeking out an astronomer in that sparse, straggling group of women and men. "Is that one an astronomy professor?" he'd ask, his voice cracking high with speculation, and I'd have to answer: "No, he's in the Speech Department," or maybe it would be English, or Art, or else World Literature, or Social Welfare (of all things). What he wanted to know was about the coming death of all the stars.

"In the end, they're all going to have to lose their light," he said. He was trying to keep his sneakers in step as he talked, making a quick little double skip to get back in step again when the wrong foot appeared. "I know it was atomic physicists who found out about the energy of the sun and all the other stars," he said, "but I want to know why things as high up there as stars have to go dark again."

I didn't know anything about galaxies exhausting their supply of hydrogen, or internal atomic reactions hastening their end, but one of my students was passing by on the chanting line, talking as he always does in the ordinary course of things. His name is Heywood Haut, and he has a tough, confident way about him, and foreign travel and bright shirts to lend him a sophisticated air.

"Poetry is for the people," Woodie Haut was saying so clearly and unequivocally that even the Tactical Squad could hear him. "And it should represent the people. If the academic and reactionary poets want to keep the art for themselves, then they're no different from the administration of this college that is trying to keep education for a select few."

"Do you think maybe astronomy's for the people?" the Chicano boy asked him, his voice sharp and high. "Do you think you could say that about astronomy, too?"

It wasn't that day, but another November day that he was arrested, some time before the real slaughter began. Until his arrest, nobody knew (or had even given a thought to it) that he wasn't a student at San Francisco State but a high school dropout from the Mission District. He said in court he'd joined the picket line because that was the closest he'd ever get to being in college.* He was sentenced for trespassing and for inciting to riot, as one of the outside agitators the college administrators, the Trustees, and the frightened State of California had come to see behind every hydrangea bush and every redwood tree.

V

On the evening of November 13th, President Smith was persuaded by a faculty delegation and student representatives to close the college. The following day, the largest faculty meeting in the history of San Francisco State filled the Main Audi-

* See page 74

torium to overflowing. A sigh of relief, a murmur of gratitude, could be heard in the packed hall as Smith announced that classes would not be resumed until tranquillity had been restored. The faculty motion "to suspend the educational facilities of the college immediately and indefinitely while faculty stay in continuous session" was adopted by a large voice vote. It was also strongly recommended that Smith request an emergency meeting with the Trustees.

The first time I laid eyes on President Smith, some months before, I mistook him for a plainclothes cop. But eventually I came to judge him as just one more flesh-and-blood symbol of the vast expanse of conviction and activity that lies on the other side of the divide from where I am. Smith's eyes see other colors, his tongue pronounces quite different words, his ears accept other nuances of speech. He, and those interchangeable men (professors, it may be, from departments of physical or mental education, or from history, or else other members of the administration) with whom he lunched at the Faculty Club, plump, graying, granite pillars of a society alien to me, were the reasons I finally could no longer bring myself to enter the club. I had been one of the charter members, but I could no longer bear to have it reaffirmed at twelve-thirty or one o'clock every day that poetry might as well cease to be written and that Verdi's *Requiem* would never again be required to soar higher and clearer and more eloquent than any other sound.

I think of Roger Alvarado, a Third World student at San Francisco State, and at the same moment I think of Robert Smith, and my mind can find no way to fit them into the same scene. There is no judgment implied in this comparison, for I have come beyond judgments in my despair. Alvarado is a long-boned El Greco Christ crossing an endless desert without sandals on his feet, wandering on a journey from dawn to dusk, and not stopping even at that destination, but moving straight on into the night, saying, "All we got to do is set the world straight, after we decide if there is such a thing." Ever since 1966 Alvarado has been walking up the mountains and down the valleys, making his way out of the discarded present, seeing something blazing in the El Greco clouds ahead that, even with flashlights, the Trustees could not hope to see. To interviewers, Alvarado has said: "If you're going to recognize yourself as a human being, then you're not going to set up priorities on the basis of anybody else's. You must relate to other people's priorities from the basis of your own needs —on the basis, that is, of what you need so you don't starve physically or mentally, so you are not abused . . . Nothing pleases the other side more than when students take over a building where they can be isolated, arrested, and the impetus of the movement destroyed. Our feeling is that we don't want a mass confrontation with the cops; we don't want to have people arrested in large numbers." Alvarado was sentenced to a hundred days in jail for his part in the organization of a nonviolent rally on campus. Nearly five hundred students were

27

arrested that day, and I think of his line of poetry saying: "Don't make too much noise you might wake up the middle class."

VI

At a second overflow faculty meeting on November 15th, Dr. S. I. Hayakawa, a part-time professor in the English Department, was among those who waited to speak at the microphone in the left-hand aisle that was designated for dissent. This uneasy little man appeared more nervous than usual and he fidgeted with the notes he held as he denounced in a high-pitched, querulous voice "the black students who are again disrupting the campus" and condemned the teachers who "defend these disruptive elements." Hayakawa's own "Renaissance Group" of conservative academics, as well as faculty of the Business School and the Department of Physical Education, enthusiastically hailed his distorted presentation of one of the crucial world issues of our time. But Hayakawa, never a man of poise despite the blandness of his features, appeared shaken by the outbursts of disapprobation in the auditorium when he called for an immediate reopening of the college by whatever means might be required.

To the majority of assembled teachers, it seemed that momentous changes might be beginning, and Hayakawa's demand that the violence of the past week be continued, and even intensified, was unworthy of serious notice. President Smith himself had said that "one of the keys to dealing with the demonstrators is to be able to respond to the basic needs that underlie their [the students'] behavior, and not to their specific actions." Smith had also admitted to newsmen that the appearance of police on campus had been a mistake. Surely no one in the convocation hall on November 15th could have imagined that in the weeks ahead Hayakawa, as Acting President of the college, would be making headline news.

On Monday, November 18th, a large delegation of faculty, students, and administrators attended the emergency Trustee meeting in Los Angeles. On the 19th, another packed faculty meeting heard the report of the even further embittered men and women who had met with the Trustees the previous day. It was the specific actions of the striking students that had been the concern of the Trustees at that Los Angeles meeting. The demands of the BSU and TWLF were brushed aside, as was the statement of a student president from San Jose College who was permitted to speak to the board. He said there could be no resolution of the problem on the California campuses until there was a realization of the threat to higher education that problem presented, and until a re-evaluation was made of the state's politics, economy, and obligations. But this re-evaluation must be preceded by an assessment of the role of the student in the institution. "The student revolution has become just that—a revolution—when it could have been an evolution," he said. But the Trustees gave no sign that they had heard him speaking to them. One Trustee announced that there would never have been any trouble if the college had been run "like a business"; and another Trustee said: "Down, Rover," to a black faculty member who had touched his arm during the meeting. Nor would these men have heard the clear voice of a San Francisco ex-police lieutenant, Dante Andreotti, had he told them, as he told many other men during his twenty-seven years on the force: "You must understand that poverty does not just relate to an economic living standard, but it relates as well to a poverty of power, a poverty of belonging, and a poverty of being in the mainstream."

In the first week of December, the headlines began. HAYAKAWA STALKS OUT OF BLACK MEETING IN HUFF, announced the *Sun-Reporter* of December 7, 1968. HAYAKAWA STAGES A WALK-OUT AT KQED, said the *Sun-Reporter* of December 14th; and in the same issue, HAYAKAWA GOES MAD. On January 17, 1969, *The Daily Gater* quoted Hayakawa in a headline: "WHY, I CAME TO THIS CAMPUS TO BE WITH THE LOWER CLASSES." And the *San Francisco Chronicle* of February 15th reported in two-inch type: BLACKS, HAYAKAWA YELL AT EACH OTHER. But that day in November, when he had nervously approached the microphone, we had all failed to see him as one of the last remaining relics of all that is dead and done for forever on the campuses of America. Nor did we see him then as the perjured witness in defense of academic crimes against humanity that none of us, neither teachers nor students, can keep silent about any more.

VII

When I reached Frankfurt, Germany, on a bitter, sleeting night just before Christmas 1968, I was met by friends who were teaching at the university there. I was returning to a city I had known well immediately after World War II, and the men I knew who were now professors had been students then. In the trunk of their car were the white metal helmets they were now wearing on the picket line to protect their skulls from police batons, and the crossed sticks of their placards that said in German almost exactly what my placard had said at San Francisco State: STAND WITH US FOR A UNIVERSITY FREE FROM POLITICAL TYRANNY! These men had gone out on strike in support of student demands and student grievances, as we had at State, and the Christmas holidays were no more than a momentary pause in the long walk we had undertaken on different continents without prearrangement or conspiracy.

The German students I spoke to that first night at the Club Voltaire wanted to know one thing above all else: what was the political orientation of the striking faculty and students at San Francisco State? In America, this question could have half a dozen different implications, but in Europe it meant one thing: Are you, all of you, even the Students for a Democratic Society, willing to sacrifice every institution, every fixed belief, every habit of the mind and will, every standard and goal that has been made familiar to you in a wholly materialistic society, so that an effective re-evaluation of that society can be brought about? As one more piece of evidence of the sickness of that society, they told me of a German student, a girl of nineteen, who had taken part in a demonstration for peace in Vietnam. The demonstration had involved the burning of consumer goods in a Frankfurt department store, and she was now serving a three-year sentence for the crime of calling helpless, hopeless attention to the fact that the destruction of goods, of material objects, is an outrage to the citizenry, while the destruction of life in Vietnam is a condonable act. They asked me, these students, if I believed that a limited protest made in America (such as the protest of the academic world) could bring about social change. I said I was afraid it could not, and I wanted to be a part of their legitimate and passionate concern, as I had been when I had lived for four years in Frankfurt, but I was thinking with an almost incommunicable hope of other things.

To speak of the Peace and Freedom Party to them was no answer to their questions. But discussion about the party did establish that the coalition of blacks and whites on that particular platform had marked a turning point in race relations here. Eldridge Cleaver, running as Presidential candidate on the Peace and Freedom Party ticket, said in an interview before the elections:

> Now is the time for whites to help us get the machinery together, to organize themselves and then form coalitions with black groups and Mexican and Puerto Rican groups that also want to bring about social change . . . What can whites do? Just be Americans . . . Just stand up for liberty everywhere . . . especially right here in their own country. It would be a great help for white people to start their own local organizations or to form local chapters of the Peace and Freedom Party . . . That kind of organized activity is really the only hope for this country.

My mind was also with my student Victor Turks, who had intended to write a poem (for he is a poet), but who wrote instead "An Open Letter to the Administration":

> The velocity of the black man's yearning for a situation in which he can study and learn about himself and the society in which he lives is felt by all of us. We all sense the pressure of the black man's passion. We cannot but lose balance in the presence of his frenzied momentum toward autonomy . . . We are confronted from all sides with the black man's desire to fulfill himself in the context of a white society which has yet to fulfill itself . . . As long as white backs are turned to the black

man's just pleas (however violent those pleas may be) for a Black Studies Department dedicated to the exaltation of his own destiny, then my own position and those of my fellow whites will always remain insecure. If we recoil in distaste from the disturbances taking place on our campus, it is because the very foundations of our white souls are being questioned.

I was thinking of Sartre speaking for the dead Frantz Fanon, saying that all the terrible, inexcusable, uncondonable acts of violence committed by those at bay are neither empty sound and fury, nor the resurrection of savage instincts, but are part of the anguished process of Man recreating himself. Whether he knew these words or not, Victor's letter continued as if he did:

> . . . I see American blacks as a lively, redeeming force, men moving through life with a poetic force and a clear-sightedness of the unjust ways of the world . . . The urgent tempo with which the black man hurls himself at life and American society dazzles us . . . The American black possesses the power to regenerate this white society . . . We should accept the black man's advances toward self-possession as a gesture of salvation. Let the black man rejoice in his dignity as a human being. Let *him* for once—not the white man, not Europe, not Western civilization—set the example for all to follow.

In January 1969, striking Nanterre students whom I met in Paris, students who had left their classrooms in protest against the distortions in the aims and teaching of social psychology, put the same urgent questions to me as had the German students. To seek to win on a purely moral basis, they argued, was asking for defeat. They themselves had gone out on strike for existential rather than ideological reasons, and they had learned, they said—and learned it through pain and disillusionment and prison terms—that it is only through politically organized action that one can overcome national and international inhumanity. They believed that American activists have not yet come to the full realization that protest isolated from the problems of the masses cannot bring about radical reform; but whether, in the end, it would be a workers' revolution, with the rebellion of the intellectuals no more than an auxiliary to the wider social upheaval, or whether it would be the intellectuals who would give that deep and wide upheaval its impetus, they were not agreed. But because of the racial issue which divides America (and despite the fact that the American working class is committed to no radical political party), they were persuaded that the United States is closer to revolution than is their own country.

Two disturbing things took place when I spoke in early January at the American Center for Students and Artists in Paris. The first occurred during the question period, when a man—an American—stood up in the audience to say that even though I had taught my San Francisco College students in my home during November and December, in those intervals when I was not on the picket line, I had certainly not taught them what the State of California had hired me to teach. "You have declared here that you gave those students the grade of A if they made clear that they understood the issues of the strike and wrote about those issues," he said. "That is not the subject you were hired for." French students, of whom there were many in the hall, booed his remarks, and another American leapt up to say that surely it was my responsibility to teach my students many things, among them an ability to make their own choices intelligently. When I said that I gave my students A's for their comprehension of the realities of the struggle in which we were engaged, the first American protested even more vigorously. "If you had been in one of my classes," I said when he was done, "I would have had to give you an F for lack of comprehension." This brought about such applause that I felt I had been hasty and unjust, and I wanted to make amends for my words.

The second incident was this: After my talk, a young American Indian woman, perhaps a student, shouted her dark and terrible anger at me as I came down from the stage. I had spoken of the black man's and the artist's loneliness and persecution and despair, she cried out, but not one word had I said about the Indian's plight, about the acts of genocide which had wiped fifty million American Indians from their own land. "Are we on the reservations ever told that we have the right to an education, that there are scholarships available to us? Are we ever told that we have a right to escape our prison, to function as free women and men?" I stood silent before this American Indian crying out for justice in the strange setting of an American cultural center in Paris, France; and then one of the French students in the group of them who had gathered around us shouted out: "*Imbécile!* What are you doing staying over here?"

These two aggrieved Americans who filled the hall with the pain of their own truths haunted me from that night on. I wanted to take them, both girl and man, back to San Francisco with me, but she had run out onto the Boulevard Raspail, and I could see her moving in agitation out of the green-white cone of one street-light into the next, her hair like a wild pony's mane, talking, gesticulating, with French students following and encircling her. I wanted her to hear the Shoshonean on the picket line on Nineteenth Avenue as he paraphrased Thomas Merton, telling me that the ultimate surrender of the Indian is to believe himself a being who belongs on a reservation, and that he must remain there in order to preserve the identity the white man has invented for him; or saying that the aboriginal owners of the United States can never sell themselves to the white man as fully human because of the white man's impossible terms. Or to hear the voice of another young Indian saying:

"My name is Clyde Warrior and I'm a full-blood Ponca Indian from Oklahoma. In the old days the Ponca people lived on the buffalo and we went out and hunted it. We believed that God gave the buffalo as a gift to us. That did not erode our character, for no one went out and found the buffalo for us and no one organized our hunts for us, nor told us how to divide our meats, nor told us how to direct our prayers. We did that ourselves. And we felt ourselves to be a competent, worthy people. In those days, we were not 'outside the system.' We were the system, and we dealt competently with our environment because we had the power to do so. The epitome of democracy is responsibility as individuals and as communities of people. There cannot be responsibility unless people can make decisions and stand by them or fall by them."

But the American to whom I had given an F for lack of comprehension, perhaps hoping to catch me in *flagrante delicto,* agreed reluctantly to come with me. We returned by way of Frankfurt, and together we sat in a German home one night of our journey and watched the TV commemoration program of the fiftieth anniversary of the murder by the military of Rosa Luxemburg and Karl Liebknecht. Sitting there in the dark of the *Wohnenzimmer,* we listened to Rosa Luxemburg saying: "Can anyone 'explain' what Mozart's music is? Can anyone 'explain' of what the magic of life consists if the smallest and most matter-of-fact things don't tell him—or, better, if he doesn't have this magic in him?" And for the moment we forgot the things we had been thinking of each other, for in a little while Rosa Luxemburg would be battered to death before our eyes by members of the *Freikorps*.

On the picket line that stretched from Holloway along Nineteenth Avenue, the American witness from Paris might well have been reassured. One of the greatest experts on the work of Samuel Beckett walked casually there day after day, mile after mile, talking of modern German opera, holding high a placard which read: EDUCATION, NOT REGIMENTA-TION! And a teacher of the Victorian novel, bearing a sign that declared his current commitments and beliefs, quoted the poetry of Hardy as he walked. With us marched as well a Japanese-American professor of anthropology armed with the handsomely lettered statement: WE ORIENTALS MAY ALL LOOK ALIKE, BUT WE DON'T THINK ALIKE. And an Asian student carried a sign on which Hayakawa's photograph appeared, with the inscription: TOJO IS ALIVE AND WELL AND LIVES IN MARIN COUNTY.

The students who walked with us knew one thing well: that had their teachers sought to face the issues of war, of genocide, of famine, of racial fury, of nuclear annihilation, which had brought us all to where we were, they would not have had to put down their books and set out to march in defiant masquerade, in broken-heeled cowboy boots, or in sandals, or barefoot, across the campuses of state after state, land after land. There they were, our long-haired, tattered, chanting army, asking of us who had flung them out of the playpen of childhood into the fire of napalm and the tears of mace, that something be done, that some world-wide action be taken, to save them from the floundering adult universe that differed so little from limbo or from hell.

VIII

The American I had brought back through conscience from Paris with me early in the new year I now dragged up and down the picket line day after day, fair weather or foul. He spoke to no one, asked no questions, and if references were made to the horror of all that had taken place here in November and December, he showed no sign of interest. He looked neither right nor left as he walked, but straight ahead, as the silent majority doubtless walks, his eyes fixed on the unshaken conviction that none of us, since the beginning of the strike, had taught our students what the State of California had hired us to teach. He may have believed that the English Department was teaching astronomy, and the Art Department was giving courses in race relations, and that the Speech Department had abandoned eloquence for the instruction of karate or mime. It sometimes occurred to me that he was a member of the CIA, for when I tried to touch him he was not there.

He did not join in the singing—not in "We Shall Overcome" or "Solidarity Forever" or "I'm

Stickin' with the Union"—and when the guerrilla theater acted out its plays on the steps of the college buildings, he did not seem to see the shower of phoney greenbacks which the figure labeled "Chicago Billionaire" flung out in handfuls to a small man in a tam-o'-shanter who wore a lei of grotesque paper orchids around his neck. The day after Hayakawa told the press that the protesting students and many of their teachers were high as kites on dope, one elderly professor brought a yellow kite to the picket line, and the marchers broke ranks to help him sail it into the wind above the trees. But the American from Paris was not among those who helped to launch it, nor did he appear to see Hayakawa's likeness painted on it, with the legend HAYAKAWA, HIGHER THAN A KITE. Nor was he moved by the passivity of one of my Chinese students who, when the police were looking the other way for a moment, read his poem in a low voice to me as we walked:

> I'll be a poet in exile
> having learned—especially from your spirit
> that the hand must be a clenched firm fist
> against injustice.
>
> But you must feel also the pulsating
> of the blood in the firm fist
> for the heart and life line
> are at the very center of it.

And another time, Shawn Wong (whose forefathers had sometimes been awakened at night by the falling of a lotus petal from a vase across the room), after the mounted police had charged and trampled students under the horses' panic-stricken hooves, wrote a poem about what had taken place:

> I thought of the small white flowers
> trampled in the grasses
> and the blood of poets lying near
> the broken stems.

But the American, whose name I never learned, and whose face I did not lay eyes on even for a moment, remained untouched. I imagined that grey hairs sprang from the pores in his neck, and bristled in bunches in the hollows of his ears, but it seemed to me that these hairs did not leap from his skin in lively curiosity about the young or in hope for what might lie ahead. So I wrote out a little romance of events for him in order that the blood would stir with youth in his veins again. The first chapter began:

> The word "power" is a disquieting word to the citizens of the most powerful country in the world. And, knowing that, you know that the more familiar term "Black Power" is less frightening than the cry "Power to the People!" It was a cry that dismayed many members of the faculty seated in the Main Auditorium of San Francisco State on the morning of November 20, 1968. A public dialogue between student leaders, faculty, and members of the administration was about to get under

way. As representatives of the Third World and the Black Students Union walked down the crowded aisle to the stage, black men raised their clenched right fists and shouted: "Power to the People!"

Bleak terror put on the guise of irritation, and here and there in the packed hall that morning, men in good grey suits ran their forefingers under the collars of their white shirts, and a few of the panic-stricken rose and left the auditorium.

I had always conceived of the suit of this American who walked with me as being grey, and drearily cut, similar to those of the professors who had walked out of the hall. His shirt, like theirs, must have been so much a status symbol that he need not have expressed his opinion on any subject, inasmuch as everything had already been clearly stated. But I kept believing it was in my power to reveal to him some redeeming secret he had not suspected the existence of before.

"Perhaps you would have walked out with the others," I said, "but then your ire would have been aroused by the sound of violins grinding out *Moments Musicaux* in the Music Department's soundproof cubicles, and you would have wanted to break down the doors to stop the cadenzas spiraling up and down the same old coloratura staircases when the fate of San Francisco State was hanging in the balance."

But still he could not, or anyway did not, answer, and so I began the second chapter of the little book that would tell him in a nutshell what had taken place.

There was great uneasiness in the auditorium the day the convocation opened. Mayor Alioto had come early to the campus to confer with Smith and been jeered by the massed students, who eventually escorted him off campus. "I was only trying to help," he muttered as he got into his car. In Los Angeles, the Trustees were clamoring for the reopening of classes, and pressuring Smith to call in the police.

At times it was the angry accusations of the Black Students Union representatives at the panel table that an audience of several thousands listened to on closed-circuit television; at other times, it was the forbearing reasoning of administration officers and faculty mediators. As this labored exchange continued, the white man's vocabulary declined from high-flown rhetoric to uneasy soliloquy. There was no recognition of the other's thought on that platform, and every statement underscored the irreconcilable prejudices of both the white and the nonwhite worlds. The black men were reduced to speaking their vast truths in a language of obscenities and violent abuse. The white men still uttered vowels and consonants, but the words they thought so highly of were already obsolete. The astonishing fact was that in this unprecedented moment of confrontation, when black and yellow and white men were seated as equals at a table on a stage, and looking at long last into one another's eyes, the white men were caught singularly unprepared. Where they had been for all their lifetimes, one did not know, but in this perilous instant of history they sat before their accusers with no defense to offer except one it was impossible to voice: that they had never believed things would be allowed to go this far.

But now the story of what took place had acquired such serious proportions that I could no longer take the time to write it down. The end came on November 26th, I told the American from Paris, speaking urgently, urgently, in the hope that he would finally understand. President Smith's resignation was announced from Los Angeles, and half an hour later S. I. Hayakawa had been named Acting President of San Francisco State. His first official act was to close the college a day before the Thanksgiving holiday was to begin. "Neither the closing nor the 'state of emergency' regulations Hayakawa put into effect had anything to do with finding a language we could all speak," I said, trying to tell the story rationally. "Those laws meant the proscribing of all communication. The use of the speaker's platform was subject to Hayakawa's approval, and the same restriction applied to sound equipment." I quoted an editorial from *The Daily Gater* which pointed out that by closing the school Hayakawa had obliterated any flickering hope that the convocation held for a resolution of the problems of the college, for the convocation had provided the closest contact between administrators and strikers since the strike began. After these edicts, it was only the long march of the disillusioned that one witnessed, and the outcry of the despairing that one heard.

As a member of the press, I had heard Hayakawa say at his first press conference in November (a conference from which faculty, as such, were excluded) that he hoped the teachers and students at San Francisco State would feel threatened by him, for that was what he intended. He spoke at that time of the $100,000 check which his friend, Chicago multibillionaire W. Clement Stone, had sent him, along with a bushel basket of orchids from Hawaii. It might be possible to start a police school on campus with this money, Hayakawa said, and in this way students and faculty would come to see that policemen, too, are human beings. He said more money would be forthcoming, which would enable him to implement the programs he wanted to put through: among them, flower beds all over the campus, and music in front of the cafeteria, so that San Francisco State College would become again the "swinging campus" that he had known in 1955. ("In dealing with these wonderful Negro people," Clement Stone once said in an interview, "you have to get them to laugh, to relax, enjoy it— and then give them hope." *) When Stone sent his congratulations to Hayakawa for his handling of campus disorders, and added that the way to deal with rebellious students was to make them fear

* As quoted in *The Nation*, March 17, 1969.

"they are going to be incarcerated and stay there," he was speaking for many in our bitterly divided society.

Now it was January, and teachers and students had been marching for better than two months. For a time, neighboring churches had offered their meeting halls and conference rooms for both striking and nonstriking students to attend their classes out of reach of the police. With only twenty percent of the student body crossing the picket lines to enter the college, direct action politics had begun to impress even the most moderate of our associates. But as campus and community unrest intensified, public pressure was brought on the ministers, and the church doors were one after another closed. My house is large, and five professors (from the English, World Literature, and International Relations Departments) were provided with keys, and between picketing duty we met our classes there. We saw our students for longer periods, and in many instances more frequently than we had in our classrooms, for without willing it, and without wholly understanding it, we had become outcasts together, and the old artificial barriers were no longer there. Black, oriental, white, and Mexican, we were resisting together the armed invasion of a territory we knew was entirely our own.

Even my student Richard Rebhun put aside his armor of arrogance for a moment and wrote: "There are times when we make decisions, and revel in the fact that we have become men. Each time the baton falls on an innocent head, the pain is felt by all of us. This is the beginning of wisdom. If you wish to see mankind, look into the mirror. If you look long enough, one man will become ten men, and then a hundred men, and soon a tide of hope will be reflected in the glass. This strike is a philosophical expression of Man's eternal search, and behind any physical manifestations of our fervor can be heard the cry that a world must be built in which we are less tools of an immensely impersonal power and more men of flesh and blood."

And my student Father James Hietter wrote that January: "Christian hate has gone for so many centuries by the name of love that it is time we called it by its right name."

IX

One evening, after a late class in my home, I took out a few pages from my diary, and I gave them to the mute American witness to read. The first entry was dated December 2, 1968, and it began:

> When I arrived at the college this morning there was a sound truck parked by the curb on Nineteenth Avenue. It was not yet eight, but the moving line of picketing students was already two blocks long. They were chanting "On strike! Shut it down! On strike! Shut it down!" while an amplified voice from the parked truck exhorted students to stay out of their classrooms until the fifteen demands of

their disadvantaged brothers had been met. No police were visible for the moment, but I knew they were in the halls of every building, and that they were massed in the cellar of the gym. By eight o'clock, undercover agents in black twill raincoats would be at our heels wherever we moved.

And then the amplified voice abruptly stopped speaking, and students were crowding around the sound truck and crying out in protest. On top of the truck was a whirling, irate little man, wearing a tam-o'-shanter, a plump little figure who was tugging and leaping and close to foaming at the mouth in his paroxysm of rage. I moved in closer with the students, who were now calling out: "Freedom of speech, Dr. Hayakawa! What about freedom of speech?" Others were laughing at the sight, and admonishing him: "Now, remember, no violence, no violence! We can't have anything like that!"

But the Acting President of the college was pushing and shoving at those who mounted the truck, including newsmen, and clawing furiously at the sound truck's wires. Once he had jerked them out, he swung around to the crowd, and, like a demented orchestra conductor, with arms and hands savagely beating out the rhythm, in furious mockery he led the students in the chant of "On strike! Shut it down!" (Later, still shaken, he told the press: "I can't stand that mindless chanting!")

I thought at once of a little man sitting in the prisoner's dock in Israel, who, when faced with the enormity of his crime, could only say that he had done what he had been ordered to do. I stood close to the truck, which was student-owned, and the owners were struggling now to keep the amplifier from destruction at Hayakawa's hands. He was flinging out to right and left into the crowd his "loyal to Dr. Hayakawa" scrolls, each tied with a blue ribbon, and every now and then he dodged as a student flung the scroll back at him. He was shouting the protesters down, his voice gone shrill as a banshee's, and I called out to him as loudly as I could: "Hayakawa Eichmann!" He swung around, trembling, and demanded above the uproar to know what I had said. When I repeated the two names, he shook an agitated finger down at me. "Kay Boyle, you're fired!" he shouted.

As a helicopter clattered overhead that day, a few arrests were made, and a few windows were broken. But Hayakawa was able to say that San Francisco State College was open.

The next entry was December 3rd:

Today, students and police clashed in the most violent campus battle since Columbia. The students had called a rally at the speaker's platform, and police poured onto the campus, broke ranks, and like madmen rushed the massed students again and again, clubbing them to the ground. One newsman, aghast at what was taking place, cried out: "My God, it's worse than Chicago!" At one point, Haya-kawa, surrounded by police as he stood on the roof of the Administration Building, shouted through a loud speaker: "If you want trouble, stay right there and you'll get it!"

The students were enraged by the unprovoked attack, and more than two thousand refused to go. They fought the police with everything they could lay their hands on: chairs from the cafeteria, table legs, rocks, garbage cans. By evening, the entire leadership of the black community—moderates, liberals, radicals—had broadcast their shock and anger, and announced they would be on campus to defend their children from police brutality.

December 4th:

I had been wrong when I believed that no outside help would come to the campus. Today Dr. Carlton Goodlett (publisher and editor of *The Sun-Reporter*), Assemblyman Willie Brown, Jr., the Reverend Cecil Williams, and other black leaders led several thousand students from an "illegal" rally at the speaker's platform up to Nineteenth Avenue, out of the reach of the police clubs. It was a stirring and completely rational statement that Dr. Goodlett, when raised to the shoulders of black administrators of the college, called out through the bullhorn. "Follow us!" he said. "We shall leave this campus to Hayakawa and the Tactical Squad!" Equally strong and clear were the words he spoke directly to Hayakawa. "The black community," he said, "is not going to permit the black students to be isolated on this campus." He said that their elders had lived for a long time and were fully prepared to give their lives in defense of their children.

Dr. Goodlett warned that "if nonviolent tactics fail, I and the other black community leaders will bear in mind the constitutional provision which gives citizens the right to bear arms." A sociologist in the group of these leaders told the press that "the black students have captured the imagination of the entire black community, and we have no choice but to support them. . . . From now on, the Governor, the Trustees, Mayor Alioto, and Hayakawa will be arrayed against not only militant students and discontented faculty but against the aroused black community as well."

December 5th:

Dr. Goodlett was arrested on campus as he informed the Tactical Squad, again through a bullhorn, that the marching students (again several thousand strong) had the right to assemble peacefully around the speaker's platform. From the top of the Administration Building, the warning was broadcast that the rally was an "unlawful" assembly and that the crowd should immediately disperse. But police action followed so closely on the announcement that many who sought to leave could not do so. The Tactical Squad, supported by regular police units, moved in on us in four flying wedges, cutting off every avenue of escape. The police charged students and speakers, jerked Dr. Goodlett down from the shoulders of his companions, and moved with clubs swinging into the panic-stricken crowd. Two white clergymen were knocked to the ground and severely beaten, and dozens of fleeing students and a number of black community leaders were clubbed. After having been booked at the police station (with twenty-five others) on charges of unlawful assembly, failure to disperse, disturbing the peace, and trespassing, Dr. Goodlett was released on his own recognizance and proceeded directly to Stockholm, where he was scheduled to address an international peace conference.

One of the saddest things in the world today was to hear our own voices singing "Hold the fort for we are coming!" as we marched, shaken, with our placards on Nineteenth Avenue.

From then on there were almost daily arrests of students and faculty, followed by the retaliatory smashing of windows and plate glass doors. Fifteen nonstriking department chairmen sent a telegram to the Secretary of the San Francisco Labor Council, urging that strike sanction be accorded Local 1352 so that an end might be brought to the intolerable situation at the college. "A sanctioned AFT strike, leading to a temporary but orderly closing down of the campus," the telegram read in part, "seems necessary to achieve a breakthrough." An entry in my diary, dated December 7th, noted that one of the largest community meetings to be held in post-war years by the Japanese-American citizenship of San Francisco was called to discuss the crisis. One hundred and seven Japanese-American students from San Francisco State were present at the meeting, as well as four nisei instructors. Two resolutions were passed by a majority vote. The first urged Hayakawa to take immediate action to accept unequivocally the fifteen demands of the Third World Liberation Front and the Black Students Union. The second condemned Hayakawa's methods of handling the strike, and condemned the man himself as "a tool of the power structure."

I sat looking in something like hope at the American from Paris as he put the pages down. But inasmuch as he was not there, he made no comment, gave no sign. I told him, as if in some craven way to assure him of our enormous popularity, that once Labor Council strike sanction had been accorded us, contingents of the Longshoremen's Union came to picket with us, on one occasion numbering two hundred and fifty strong. From then on, employment on the docks was open to those striking teachers who were in good enough physical condition to undertake loading cargo. One late afternoon soon thereafter, seven hundred and fifty Bay Area elementary school teachers joined our picket line, I told him, and presented our Local with a check for $1,300. Salaries of the striking teachers had ceased, while the police units at the college were costing the taxpayers of the city the staggering sum of $30,000 a day.

San Francisco State's Academic Senate, I confided to the American from Paris, speaking to him now in the most wheedling of voices, had commended the AFT for its role in bringing about mediation efforts through every channel it could turn to. But these efforts had foundered on the refusal of Governor Reagan and the Trustees to enter into any productive discussions. The Labor Council informed all those in official positions who were opposed to us that the teachers' strike "was a determined and forthright insistence on having a voice in the decisions that shape their lives," not adding that it was a hopelessly doomed insistence. With organized labor's sanction, I said to the American's dogged silence, our strike had ceased to be a support action of the students' grievances and a protest against the occupation of the campus by military units; for sanction had been granted Local 1352 with the clear understanding that the Labor Council did not "regard student problems as labor strike issues." But however that may have been, faculty and student picket lines continued in a single dense line on Nineteenth Avenue, and the songs the students sang with us were still "Solidarity Forever," and "Joe Hill," and "I'm Stickin' with the Union."

It was the end of January now, and I might have brought my commitment to this man from Paris to an end by accepting the fact that he was without existence had not a singular thing happened one cold rainy day. It was another day of mass arrests, and the paddy wagons roared one after another in swift succession up the campus walk that we now called Death Alley. As they swung around the picket line, I could see the faces of students through the meshed glass at the back windows, and their bloodied fingers lifted in the "V" of victory.

It was perhaps when the fourth or fifth evil black van came speeding up the walk that I felt an urgent, confident hand take hold of mine. It might have been that we had talked about this action we were about to take, and together come to a decision, but we had not talked of it. Yet without a tremor of hesitation we walked out of the picket line and stood, hand grasping hand, before the oncoming patrol wagon. For an instant I saw the blanched, stricken face of the policeman behind the wheel, and then I closed my eyes, and my bones went weak with fear. I shook off the hand that was still holding mine, and I took the two cowardly steps backward to safety, and left the American who had come so far standing there quite alone.

That was the end. He was never present in my life again. But nothing appeared in the papers about what must have taken place, and no one I spoke to had ever heard of a middle-aged man being struck down as he stood in the way of a paddy wagon that was carrying students off to jail. But I knew he had taken the only way that was left to him, not to die, but merely to be able to survive.

X

To survive. To make it somehow with dignity, and yet to eat and have a roof over one's head.

One striking secretary (who subsequently lost her job) described in an open letter to the administration the situation as it applied to all of us. She wrote:

> In an attempt to discover my right to be free from danger of physical attack while on this campus, I called every board and agency from the National Labor Relations Board on down. I found that I have no rights and the state has no responsibilities. The state is exempt from its own laws. There *is* redress of grievances. The state handles it. If you claim that the state has unjustly withheld your pay, or unjustly dismissed you, or been remiss in its duties or responsibilities, the state decides, through the State Personnel Board, whether the state has been so remiss. The State Personnel Board is a state agency, working for the state, and it decides whether you have a grievance against the state.

The truths expressed in this letter are relevant to a hearing which was scheduled to take place on the evening of April 24, 1969, before a panel of the Committee of Grievance and Disciplinary Action at San Francisco State. Four months before, Dr. Arthur Bierman, of the Philosophy Department, had requested the Committee investigate Hayakawa's actions to determine if he was guilty of unprofessional conduct. I had also asked the Committee to take under consideration my complaint against Hayakawa's actions, and his precipitant dismissal of me, on the sound truck on the morning of December 2, 1968. The two cases were combined and summarized in the following articles:

1. Hayakawa accepted the Acting Presidency knowing he was violating campus procedure for selection of presidents.
2. He failed to notify the Faculty Presidential Selection Committee that he was a candidate for Acting President.
3. He broke a solemn agreement with the other members of the committee that no person would be a candidate while a member of the committee.
4. He acted in an intemperate, undignified way by damaging private property, attempting to seize private property, and shoving persons physically.
5. He acted in a hasty, ill-tempered, and irresponsible manner by "firing" Kay Boyle on the spot.

This is not the language of poets; but civilized custom demands that even the most fervent convictions, the purest of philosophies, be reduced to technical terms and be given lesser labels before either conviction or philosophy can be recognized and weighed. It was not for Hayakawa's ruthless violation of the spirit of Man, or his betrayal of the socially rejected and despised, that he could be asked for an accounting. He was to be judged for the violation of prescribed laws of professional conduct; nor could it be made clear that it was not for a moment one man's acts and words that were to be scrutinized, but those of all the panic-stricken men and women who, faced with the threat of social change, menaced by the prospect of equality with the outcast, believed he spoke for them.

Hayakawa, in an effort to avert the April 24th hearing, had the following letter (dated March 12, 1969) delivered to me by hand.

> Dear Kay Boyle:
> I once told you—and I am willing to say again—that I am happy to be the colleague of a writer as distinguished as yourself. I am sorry that profound differences of opinion have now troubled our relations.
> You say that during the sound-truck incident of December 2nd, you called me "Hayawaka-Eichmann." I did not hear you because of the level of surrounding noise. I hope you will believe me, therefore, when I tell you that I did not say to you at that time, "Kay Boyle, you are fired." I do not have the power to "fire" you or anybody else. I knew it then and I know it now. What I actually said was, "Kay Boyle, you should be ashamed of yourself."
> Shall we both, therefore, set the record straight on what we said to each other that morning? And then let's forget it.
> > Sincerely,
> > Don

On March 16th, I replied as follows:

> Dear Dr. Hayakawa:
> Your letter of March 12th is before me. In this letter you suggest that we forget the incident which occurred on December 2, 1968.

Your suggestion is inconceivable. The spectacle of a college president, his emotions completely out of control, violently attacking a privately owned vehicle on a public thoroughfare is not a sight that can be easily forgotten. Nor can I manage to forget the words you shouted at me at that time.

The scene you created was a disgraceful one, of a kind that you are constantly condemning in public statements. But far graver than this, you were by your actions at that time attacking the right of freedom of speech. The abridgment of that right you have enforced by any and all means that have been placed at your disposal. If I were to forget your firing me on December 2nd, at a moment when you clearly had no conception of what you were saying, I would then have to forget your betrayal of the academic community since you accepted the office of Acting President of San Francisco State College.

I would have to forget the unjustifiable police violence you brought to our campus, and the sight of my students' battered faces. I would have to forget all the shocking terms you have used on numerous occasions to describe the motives and the characters of those faculty members who oppose your views and deplore your actions. I would have to forget the suppression of campus publications and the violation of democratic principles on every level which you have brought about in compliance with the directions of those in political authority.

I am more than willing to admit that my lack of courtesy in calling you Eichmann on December 2nd cannot be justified by the accuracy of that name. But there are moments when courtesy becomes a questionable shelter from the violence of reality. The violence in every sense of the word was entirely on your part on that day. Because of this fact, I feel it should now be you who makes a conciliatory gesture on behalf of our college. I am more than willing to give no more thought to the incident in question if you will demonstrate your good will by extending amnesty to the students at San Francisco State (including Mason Wong*), and to those on our faculty who are to be unjustly removed from their positions.

Sincerely,
Kay Boyle

So the hearing took place. Art Bierman and I had asked for an open hearing, but the accused has the right of choice, and Hayakawa specified that the hearing be closed. It began at seven in the evening, lasted three hours, and included a television news film to support our charges. Hayakawa did not attend, but—to quote from the record of the panel —"sent a letter which was read by his delegated representative; no evidence in the form of witnesses or testimony was presented to refute the charges." Members of the Presidential Selection Committee were among our witnesses; others, who had been

* See page 91

present on the morning when Hayakawa ripped out the wires of the sound system on the student's truck, had heard the words he screamed out as he whirled in rage.

On May 22nd, the Hearing Committee recommended, by a vote of four to one, that disciplinary action be taken against Hayakawa, as the evidence appeared "to indicate clearly that the accused acted without consideration for established campus procedures in accepting the Acting Presidency of the college; that the behavior of the accused in 'attacking' the sound truck and the immediate events relating to that attack were not consistent with the office which the accused has just assumed; that the ill-advised remark made to Professor Boyle was a violation of due process." The panel further recommended that Hayakawa "vacate the office of Acting President of San Francisco State College as soon as possible and that he instruct the Faculty Presidential Selection Committee to provide a replacement for him by accepted procedure." But Hayakawa himself, as a representative of the State of California, with the political power of the state and the governor behind him, has the final decision as to the right of state employees to recommend that disciplinary measures be taken, or not taken, against any representative of the state; therefore no action ensued.

The strike had begun in the first week of November, and it ended in the first week in March, when the faculty accepted a settlement offered by the Trustees. Students and teachers alike, we were physically and spiritually depleted, and many of us had to borrow money on which to live. And so we had given in, in order to survive, with or without dignity. Even with the support of all those who had walked out of the college with us—the secretaries, the cafeteria workers—and those who had come from other cities and other campuses to join the picket line, we could not win. For we were opposing a force that goes far beyond the limits of one college president, one campus, one state. We were opposing a nation's fear, a fear that has brought us to the passing of ruthless judgments on our own children, and on the black man who has lived so long in the dark basement of our other selves. They have found us out, these two symbolic figures, and they will no longer do our bidding. We call on the police to subdue them, and to protect our possessions, our glass windows, our complacencies, our handful of dust, because we are mortally afraid.

EPILOGUE

In the end, we are faced by two very living figures—living, that is, until they have been annihi-
lated in one way or another by the death-oriented
forces in our society. These two figures seem at
times to be more alive than we are ourselves, for
they have had the courage to speak out for us. One
is the black man, whose voice can now be heard
after centuries of almost total silence in our country; the other is the student in revolt. The death-
oriented in our society I identify as those who
desperately resist any commitment to the science of
being. Those in metaphysical revolt I see as men
and women who are taking action against the vast
unrealities they have been given to live by. Action
in this sense (and doubtless in all senses) can be a
written word, or it can be paint on canvas, or it can

be rock and roll; and it can also be the stammering and the shouting and the weeping of those in exile and those in prison who seek to clarify the fundamental processes so that all men may at least hope to live in freedom and pride. David Hume wrote that we must cultivate true metaphysics in order to destroy the false and adulterated philosophizing which leads in the end to nothing but sophistry and illusion. He said that accurate and just reasoning was the only remedy for Man's mindless rejection of the meaning of life.

"Accurate and just reasoning" is a powerful combination of words. It shines with such clarity that many shield their eyes from a contemplation of it. But "accurate and just reasoning," Hume insisted, could enable men to subvert the abstruse metaphysical jargon which was rendering all philosophical thought impenetrable. I believe that the black man and the student in protest are now speaking a valid metaphysical language, a language that is shockingly unfamiliar to us, shaped by a determination to observe and confront the world as it actually is. And I believe that we who listen must learn to hear the new rhetoric that is on their tongues.

The writers of spirit and fervor in our country are those who signal the presence of two enormous and enormously historic figures: the dissenting student and the articulate black. The rational demand that human criteria be restored to our society, that the human responsibility of the individual be recognized—this demand is so dangerous that it has been distorted beyond recognition by the fearful and the cynical. In America, the faces of these two redeemers of our society have been publicly and hideously disfigured, not alone by the clubs of the police (which is bad enough), but also by the ruthless judgment of the threatened. It has come to the point in our country where the dictates of the heart or a reference to philosophical disciplines are looked on as forms of political subversion.

Because of these two living symbols of our failure to develop a society in which human values can prevail unchallenged, it is not easy to get on with the things we have, as individuals, disciplined ourselves to do. If one is a writer, one makes the attempt to go on with one's writing, but the black man and the student lay furious hands upon one's present and upon one's future. They have no time left for the past, these victims of America's hideous catastrophe, and their truths are more imperative than writing. Suddenly all our accepted and respected learning that served us in the past has become obsolete. Open a book in order to escape the non-negotiable demands of America's contemporary reality and you will discover that the statements by which we have ordered our lives are no longer there on the printed page. They have been effaced by the graffiti of the young; and the platitudes, the cliches, by which we have lived in comfort are now shouted from the page by the black man's manifesto which is so offensive to our well-bred ears. But the language of that manifesto is his own, and if the syntax and grammar appall us, and the content seems outrageously immoral in its violence, then it is we—not the black man—who must re-examine the meaning of morality. Remember Henry Miller saying—and saying it a long time ago—that he does not call poets those who make verses, rhymed or unrhymed? He calls that man "poet" who is capable of profoundly altering the world.

It is a wonder to me that writing has not stopped altogether. But writing at its deepest and highest points is Man's last confession, his testament, and he cannot accept to stop breathing until he has set the words of it down. John Hawkes, one of the most interesting writers in America today, said to me recently that never has the nightmare been so widespread. We—writers, artists, students—must seek to dispel this nightmare before it is too late, he said. Not too late for the buildings to soar even higher, or for the IBM machines to keep on functioning, but too late for the science of mind and spirit to prevail. The ideals that students and artists seek to make clear to those who will listen are very similar, Hawkes said, and we must hasten to bring the high school to the campus so that these ideals may more quickly find a common tongue. Writers, artists, students, all share a faith in the imagination, he said, and that commitment is indestructible. He spoke of the student revolt throughout the world as one of the greatest human expressions of the twentieth century. Ideas and energy are with the young, Hawkes said, and it is the young who will save us if it is still possible for us to be saved. And he added that he will remain faithful to fiction, for he sees fiction as more accurate and more reliable than history inasmuch as it compiles the record not only of what we were at a given moment, but also of what we may have, in our time, sought to become.

A Listing
of the Strike Demands

STUDENTS

Following is a list of the fifteen strike demands as put forth by the Black Students Union and the Third World Liberation Front.

The Ten BSU Demands

1 That all Black Studies courses being taught through various other departments be immediately made part of the Black Studies Department, and that all the instructors in this department receive full-time pay.

2 That Dr. Nathan Hare, Chairman of the Black Studies Department, receive a full professorship and a comparable salary according to his qualifications.

3 That there be a Department of Black Studies which will grant a Bachelor's Degree in Black Studies; that the Black Studies Department, the chairman, faculty, and staff have the sole power to hire faculty and control and determine the destiny of its department.

4 That all unused slots for Black Students from Fall 1968 under the Special Admissions Program be filled in Spring 1969.

5 That all Black students wishing so be admitted in Fall 1969.

6 That twenty (20) full-time teaching positions be allocated to the Department of Black Studies.

7 That Dr. Helen Bedesem be replaced from the position of Financial Aids Officer, and that a Black person be hired to direct it, that Third World people have the power to determine how it will be administered.

8 That no disciplinary action will be administered in any way to any students, workers, teachers, or administrators during and after the strike as a consequence of their participation in the strike.

9 That the California State College Trustees not be allowed to dissolve the Black program on or off the San Francisco State College campus.

10 That George Murray maintain his teaching position on campus for the 1968-69 academic year.

The Five TWLF Demands

1 That a school of Ethnic Studies for the ethnic groups involved in the Third World be set up with the students in each particular ethnic organization having the authority and control of the hiring and retention of any faculty member, director and administrator, as well as the curriculum in a specific area study.

2 That fifty (50) faculty positions be appropriated to the School of Ethnic Studies, 20 of which would be for the Black Studies Program.

3 That in the Spring semester, the college ful-

fill its commitment to the nonwhite students in admitting those that apply.

4 That, in the Fall of 1969, all applications of nonwhite students be accepted.

5 That George Murray, and any other faculty person chosen by nonwhite people as their teacher, be retained in their positions.

TEACHERS

Strike Issues of
The San Francisco State
College AFT Local

I.   Strike Issues Directed to the President and Administration at San Francisco State College:

A.   Negotiation of and adoption of comprehensive rules and regulations governing:

1.   Grievance procedures related to faculty affairs.

2.   Personnel decisions (hiring, firing, tenure, promotion, demotion, suspension, lay-off).

3.   Conditions under which pay can be reduced or docked.

4.   Sick leave and other fringe benefits.

5.   Unit and class load assignments for full and part-time faculty.

6.   Stipulation of prerogatives and delineation of authority at various administration levels.

7.   Guidelines and standards for profes-

sional perquisites (sabbaticals, travel, research leaves).

8. Faculty involvement in decisions on academic matters (curriculum selection, assignment of faculty and staff, grading, graduation requirements, determination of calendar, admission requirements).

9. Faculty involvement in decisions governing all local administrative matters (office space, parking).

10. Recovery of faculty positions bootlegged for administrative purposes.

B. Protection of Constitutional Rights

1. Amnesty for all factulty, students, and staff who have been suspended or have been subject to other disciplinary action and/or arrested, and withdrawal of outstanding warrants as a result of activity to end racism at San Francisco State College.

2. No disciplinary action for exercising constitutionally protected rights.

C. Black Students Union and Third World Liberation Front grievances must be resolved and implementation assured.

D. All agreements on the above to be reduced to a written contract.

II. Strike Issues Directed to the Trustees of the California State Colleges:

A. All agreements made with the local administrations under (I) above shall be binding upon and accepted by the Trustees.

B. Sufficient funds shall be provided from current reserve and emergency funds to:

1. Maintain the present faculty positions (this will prevent the lay-off of 100-125 faculty in the Spring Semester, 1969).

2. Gain new positions to replace those given by various departments and schools to staff a Black Studies Department and a School of Ethnic Studies.

3. Protect the revised work loads presently scheduled in many departments for Spring 1969, and assure the same for everyone who requests it.

C. Rescission of the ten disciplinary rules passed by the Trustees on November 26, 1968.

D. Approval of the Student Union plan presented by the Associated Students at San Francisco State College.

E. Cancellation of proposed changes in Title 5 that would take away student control of student body funds.

F. Recognition of college constitution that emerges from the Constitutional Convention called by the Academic Senate at San Francisco State College.

III. Strike Issues Directed to the Governor and the Legislature:

A. That a special joint committee of the California State Assembly and Senate be appointed to conduct negotiations with the State College Board of Trustees and the Union to agree on systematic and continuing financing for the proposals under I and II above and to provide the necessary increases in salary required to maintain a qualified faculty at San Francisco State College.

B. That when the special Legislative Committee, the Board of Trustees, and the Union have reached agreement, the Committee report to the next session of the Legislature so that necessary monies may be provided to put the agreement into effect.

The Master Plan
for Higher Education
in the State of California

"All recent events at San Francisco State College," one of the striking teachers was later to write, ". . . must be understood as community petitions followed by governmental response to a conflict over three questions: Who is to learn? What is to be learned? Who is to teach?"* The question of who is to learn leads directly to the issue of the discriminatory California Master Plan for Higher Education.

The Master Plan was enacted by the state legislature in 1960 (during Governor Brown's administration) and introduced a procedure known as the "tracking system." This system is theoretically designed to separate young people who fulfill the requirements of "college material" from those who are not "academically inclined." The dangers of such a concept are self-evident. But the practical purpose of the tracking system is to channel as many students as fiscal needs may require away from

* Dr. John Hunter [Department of Psychology], "The Betrayal of Public Education at San Francisco State College," a pamphlet published by the San Francisco State College Federation of Teachers, Local 1352, AFL-CIO, February 1969.

the state colleges and into the two-year junior colleges (which are supported by local taxes). In 1959–60, steadily increasing student applications to the state colleges became more than the state structure could support; but instead of increasing corporation taxes (which represent only twenty percent of California's tax revenue, while corporations control the bulk of the state's wealth), the legislature decided to solve the problem by modifying the higher education system. The existence of locally financed junior colleges was counted on to maintain the illusion that higher education was available to every young person in the state; but our junior colleges do not offer a "higher" education. They are no more than training schools for industry.

This spring, at the height of the strike at San Francisco State, the voice of a lady having her nails done firehouse red in a beauty parlor, her head under an electric dryer, spoke her mind very clearly. She said that surely a great many children of the "not so well-off" would prefer to go directly from high school into jobs where they would feel more at home (like street cleaning, or garbage collecting, or being maintenance men, she went so far as to suggest, although her voice was a little uncertain), rather than run the risk of failing in the "intellectual atmosphere" of the college classroom. "They might feel very much *out* of it if they were *pushed* into going to college," she said. "My husband and I, and actually all my husband's business associates, think it would be better not to humiliate them in that way."

Well, the children of the underprivileged in California are humiliated, whatever the color of their skins. But it is not because they have been accepted in the colleges of their state, but because they have been excluded from them. This rankling sense of humiliation is not new, and it has no territorial confines, but it lies close to the complex roots of the rebellion at San Francisco State. For the Master Plan placed the control of these colleges in the hands of Trustees, and at the same time created the Coordinating Council for Higher Education. The members of these two bodies are predominantly businessmen, and almost without exception political appointees of the governor. The chancellor of the state college system is, in turn, appointed by the Trustees.

Before the inception of the Master Plan, the state colleges were governed by the State Board of Education and the State Superintendent of Public Instruction. The admissions policy was then to accept the top seventy percent of graduating high school students into the state colleges, while the top thirty-three percent of those graduating were admitted to the universities. Under the tracking system of the Master Plan, however, only the top thirty-three percent of graduating high school students are now judged eligible for admission to the colleges, and the top $12\frac{1}{2}$ percent for admission to the universities. As a direct result of this exclusive system, black students at San Francisco State College were less than four percent of the student body in the 1968–69 academic year, while in 1960 (just before the introduction of the Master Plan) eleven percent of the students were black. The black and Third World population of the city is approximately forty percent, and thus the disproportion in representation at the college becomes tragically clear. In the autumn semester of 1969, thirty thousand qualified students were denied entrance to their state colleges, and it is predicted that this figure may be doubled by Spring 1970.

Governor Reagan's most recent appointee to the Board of Trustees is Dudley Swim, a director of the $437-million Del Monte Corporation, and National Vice-Commander of the American Legion. Trustee Charles Luckman, who introduced the resolution to open San Francisco State College at whatever cost to life and limb, is the head of a major architectural and construction firm which bears his name. Among other impressive enterprises, Luckman's company has designed and built U.S. Military and Strategic Air Command bases in Spain and Thailand, the Convair Missile and Space Facility, and the Disneyland Hotel. (There is, surprisingly enough, a black Trustee and a Trustee with a labor background. Unfortunately, he is one and the same man, and he is employed as business agent for Local 1533 of the American Federation of Government Employees.) The six bankers who sit on the Board are men who may very well have difficulty hearing the desperate cry of the disinherited for economic liberation. And these disinherited were listening when Reagan declared that higher education is not a right, but a privilege, and they know that this privilege depends entirely on the student's social status. "If he [the high school graduate in California] is a member of the black or brown communities, his chances of escaping his oppressed condition through the educational system are minimal. Nothing in the ghetto schools he has attended or in his environment has equipped him to cope with the rigid standards erected to shut him out." *

But there is other evidence to consider. There are the individual voices of blacks, orientals, Chicanos, and American Indians, saying that what is asked of them is to relate to essentially white middle-class standards instead of to their own desperate economic status and their own equally desperate educational needs. There is one Chinese-American student who does not come from the ghetto of San Francisco's Chinatown but who had hoped to prepare himself in college to be a social worker there. But in the Chinese Language Department of San Francisco State he can learn only Mandarin, while eighty-three percent of the Chinese in the United States speak Cantonese, a language which academic authorities are inclined to dismiss as "a language of the streets." Dr. Kai-yu Hsu, who in May 1969 resigned the chairmanship of the World Literature Department at San Francisco State on the grounds that he did not wish to be associated "even marginally" with S. I. Hayakawa's administration, tells me that efforts through the years to add a Cantonese class have been repeatedly frustrated by the lack of staff allocation.

* "The Decline Of Our State Colleges," a summary published by American Federation of Teachers Local 1352, AFL-CIO, January 1969.

The loyal faculty.

Bob Wax

Kay Boyle and the police in a corridor of the Administration Building on the first day of the occupation of San Francisco State College.

An intern from the Medical Committee for Human Rights praying during a student-police confrontation.

S. I. Hayakawa

John Sanford

Ted Goodman

Ted Goodman

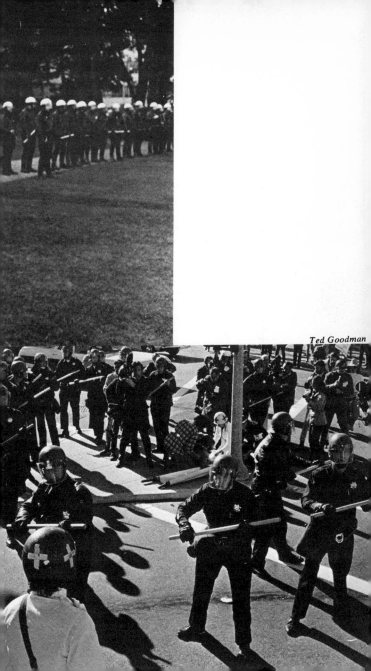

Ted Goodman

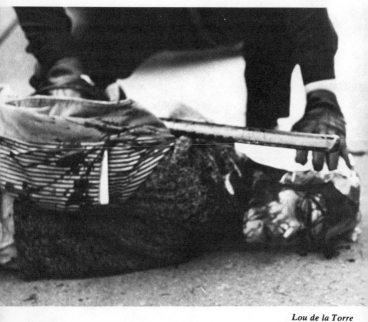

Lou de la Torre

Huey P. Newton

The co-founder of the Black Panther Party and his attorney, Charles Garry.

Lou de la Torre

A military cemetery in San Francisco

The vigil at Port Chicago.

Another Chinese student at State, Mason Wong, is an ex-Marine and a leader of Intercollegiate Chinese for Social Action, a group that is working with dedication "to keep Chinatown from exploding." While on strike, Wong said in an interview: "The Chinese people who have made it are forced to exploit their own people. Don't let the glittering lights of Chinatown fool you, because I can take you down half a block and show you communal kitchens, a community bathroom—that is, one bathroom for ninety apartments—old people in hiding because they're so poor they're afraid to come out. We can't communicate with these people because we've been educated by the white man's education. Whitewashed. Personally, I can't even speak with my own father. We've been taught to be ashamed of our own language, and of being Chinese. We have a culture, but we have no chance to learn about it . . . The reason why people love us is because we keep our mouths shut, so then they don't have to deal with us. Well, we're telling people we don't want to be loved like that any more."

In a hearing before a faculty committee in March 1969, Mason Wong, who had been arrested at a nonviolent campus rally in January, was reprimanded for his "militant" activities, suspended for six months from the college, and put on two years' probation. But in the municipal court, all charges against him were dismissed. The evidence against Wong was judged insufficient, as Hayakawa's edict banning rallies was no more than an administrative fiat and thus carried no authority as legislative act.

The Tactical Squad

The history of the Tactical Squad is brief and ignominious. Before it came into being in late 1967, riot squads were formed, when the occasion arose, from men already on the San Francisco police force. In the Spring 1964 Auto Row sit-in, such a squad dealt with demonstrators demanding an increase in minority hiring, and the squad did its job without violence. But when Joseph Alioto ran for the office of mayor, one of the strongest planks of his 1967 campaign was his emphatic dedication to "law and order." In November of that year, with Alioto elected, Police Chief Thomas Cahill promulgated General Order No. 105 "to help deal with Major Incidents and Civil Disturbances." Its general mission, according to the directive, was to provide "an immediate and mobile source of trained and equipped manpower to augment temporarily the assigned strength of a police district in the prevention and suppression of crime."

The unit is made up of thirty-four men—thirty patrolmen and four sergeants—all of whom have been selected for the job with meticulous care. Although all Tactical Squad applicants (and there is a lengthy waiting list) must pass the basic police entrance examinations, there are a number of additional requirements that must be met. In the words of Sergeant Epting of the Squad, the officers must all be "outstanding physical specimens," and he adds that "we don't want little guys." Individuality is assiduously trained out of the members of the Squad, for it is essential, for maximum effect, that they operate in action as a unit, whereas the ordinary police officer is permitted (to a degree) to function as a normal human being. Squad members also differ from the regular police force in that they receive continuous training in wrestling, judo, karate, the "proper" use of the baton, anti-sniper control, and house-to-house combat.

The Tac Squad's first confrontation with the public took place on January 11, 1968 (two months after its inception), outside San Francisco's Fairmont Hotel. This was on the occasion of Secretary of State Dean Rusk's visit to the city. Demonstrators against the war in Vietnam hurled bags of blood at the hotel. Mayor Alioto had high praise for the unit's efficiency in sweeping the street of demonstrators, cornering some in a blind alley, and kicking, beating, and slugging anyone within reach. The Squad has continuously violated, and presumably will continue to do so, the traditional role of the police officer as a keeper of the peace. With Mayor Alioto's full approval, the Tac Squad has usurped the function of a law court and metes out punishment at its own discretion and on its own responsibility.

In the summer of 1968, there was the short-lived hope that, due to public protest, the Squad might be disbanded. For on the night of July 20th, four off-duty Tactical Squad officers, who had allegedly been drinking, jumped a number of teenagers standing outside a Mission Street doughnut shop. The teenagers were black. According to eye-witness reports, the young men were, without provocation, kicked and beaten, and given the painful karate chop. One officer attempted to strangle an employee of the doughnut shop who intervened, while others beat the employee's brother who came to his defense. Two members of the Squad were subsequently suspended, and the August 3rd *San Francisco Examiner and Chronicle* described the unit as a group "operating in a fringe zone between conventional police and World War II shock troops." In the same news item it was stated that even citizens with "white, middle-class credentials sensed [in the Tactical Squad] a frightening 'paramilitary' version of their friendly police." In this instance, again, Mayor Alioto came to the defense of the Squad, pointing out that "with human nature what it is, anything can happen." The Mayor further reminded critics that "among the twelve Disciples there was one who could not be trusted." Overlooked in this statement is the fact, proven not once but over and over, that the entire Squad has been trained for this kind of action.

Opposition to the violence of the San Francisco police has been voiced by church groups, social scientists, civil libertarians, various minority organizations, and even local political figures, and also by the former head of San Francisco's Police Community Relations Unit. Dante Andreotti, a twenty-seven-year veteran of the city's police department, is now head of the municipal services section of the U.S. Department of Justice's Community Relations Service in Washington. He retired from the San Francisco police force in 1967 in despair over race relations there. In a recent interview, Andreotti said: ". . . if you invest a Tactical Squad with a gung ho kind of approach [to the community], with an almost inhuman type of image, and put them in this horrendous-looking paraphernalia some of these fellows wear today, that presents a problem. Unfortunately, the general public, as political trends now indicate, have gone along with this attitudinal posture toward increased repression of those who dare dissent." Andreotti added that "no social revolution was ever stopped by a truncheon or a bullet."

Others who speak out against this "posture toward increased repression" are the members of a newly formed organization of black San Francisco policemen. This organization is called (with modest determination) Officers for Justice, and it represents almost all of the seventy-eight black police officers in a department of seventeen hundred men. There is one white policeman in the organization, a slight young man whose moral courage is impressive. At the first public meeting of the Officers for Justice, on May 24, 1969, several hundred people, both black and white, listened with raised hopes to the officers' spoken pledge to make the black policeman in the black community "a protector of the citizenry, and not a brutal oppressor." Sergeant Henry Williams, president of the organization, said that it was not easy for black men in blue uniforms to stand up in a white police department and say to the community, "We want to help you, we want to stay any hand that will harm you." But this is what they intend to do.

Notes
on
Jury
Selection
in the
Huey P. Newton
Trial

In a three-day Suicide Interlogue sponsored last October (1967) by San Francisco State College, one set of statistics was given unusually lengthy consideration. These were statistics concerned with the high rate of nervous breakdowns and subsequent suicides among members of police forces throughout America.

It was said that it was not the fact that they were policemen that inclined them to take their own lives, but it was the result rather of that particular combination of characteristics which had led them in the first place to choose to police their fellow men.

Trained in the violent extinction of others, it was also said, it is merely another facet of the same orientation which causes them to take their service revolvers from their holsters and, frequently standing before a mirror, blow out their own brains instead of those of people whose color or class they do not like. District attorneys, concerning whom no suicide statistics are at present available, would seem by the nature of their calling to be death-oriented as well.

OAKLAND, CALIFORNIA, SITUATED ACROSS THE BAY from San Francisco, is a city of close to 400,000 inhabitants. To the eye it appears depressingly run-down, and to the ear depressingly provincial-minded. Many who live there, as well as others who cross the Bay Bridge to Oakland when necessity requires it, consider Oakland less a city than a shocking state of affairs. One earnest homeowner in the residential district said recently that "the city is long overdue for a confrontation with what is taking place throughout the world today."

That confrontation recently made legal and social history in the sensational charade of the murder trial of Huey P. Newton, twenty-six-year-old co-founder of the Black Panther Party. It was a trial that, whatever the verdict, represented one more vital step toward the clarification of the position and condition of the black community in white America. In men and women who have given little or no thought to the matter, this trial has stirred at least a partial realization that, under the present jury selection system, a black man cannot hope to be tried before a jury of his peers.

A professor at Oakland's Merritt College, a city college located on the edge of the North Oakland ghetto, put it even more strongly. "In the Newton trial, one society, one culture, is sitting in judgment on another quite alien culture and society," he said. "Newton's crime is that his skin is black."

An Oakland book dealer, who has reason to believe that his office is bugged, expressed the opinion that Oakland, to date, has come the closest of any American city—and he does not exclude the South —to being a compact working model for municipal dictatorship. "The police force of Oakland considers itself an arm of the military," this book dealer said. "Police action could at one time be described as 'protective action.' In Oakland this is no longer true. The police here have declared war on the black community, and their assaults should be recognized for what they are—actual war atrocities, complete with ambush, entrapment, and execution, either in the courtroom or outside it, of the colonized enemy." A white law student who picketed the Alameda County Courthouse during Huey Newton's trial is one of many who believes that Oakland should serve as a warning to every American city and every American citizen as to what might easily take place on a nation-wide scale.

In the hierarchy of Oakland's tight and essentially shabby dictatorship, three figures play key roles. These are Mayor John H. Reading, former

U.S. Senator William F. Knowland, publisher of the *Oakland Tribune,* and Police Chief Charles R. Gain, who has spent twenty-one years on the force and who became police chief in September 1967.

The Oakland police department, unlike that of most cities, does not have precinct stations, but instead a single headquarters housed in a large modern structure called the Police Operations Building. So bitter has become the criticism of Oakland police methods, however, that an Information Center, manned by three community relations officers in plainclothes, was opened uptown this summer. At least one of the three officers at the Center is strategically black, and the stated aim of the Center is "to get people to trust us." Militant blacks and radical whites, and a good many more conservative Oakland residents, look on the opening of this Center as an admission by the police of their own guilt, and as an unconvincing and almost ludicrous measure of dealing with a situation of great human tragedy.

With increasing exasperation, Mayor Reading has publicly stated his belief that Negro militants are not basically interested in civil rights, jobs, or better housing, but that their covert aim is political and economic control of the nation. He is strongly in favor of the use of Mace "as an effective crowd control device," and he saw to it that the temporary ban on its use by the Oakland police was speedily lifted. At a recent Oakland City Council meeting, irate citizens demanded that Reading hand in his resignation because of his failure "to understand the ferment in the black community." Black parents of teenagers who had been brutalized by the police presented their complaints, and a field representative of the Urban League voiced the view of many Oakland minority groups when he shouted at Reading: "You have evidence before you that there is a serious problem in this city, as there is in cities throughout our nation. You may not like Negroes, and this is perhaps why you cannot comprehend those who are active in behalf of black people. You just do not hear or understand the Eldridge Cleavers and the Huey Newtons."

Publisher Knowland, born and bred in Alameda County, ran for Governor of California in 1958, with a hopeful eye on an eventual Presidential campaign, but lost. In the bolted door of his *Tribune* offices a peekhole has been placed. This peekhole, Knowland stated in a recent interview, was deemed necessary after the Black Panthers, in May 1967, entered the State Capitol Building carrying guns. A gun control bill was then being discussed in the state legislature and this demonstration, during which not a shot was fired, was intended to symbolize the right of black people to bear arms in self-defense. But Knowland is not interested in the symbolic interpretation of this or any other political gesture, and in a recent statement he referred to picketing as "a form of extortion."

Police Chief Gain, who like Knowland also grew up in Oakland, called a press conference last April for the sole purpose of blasting the Black Panther Party as well as those whites who support the Panthers. When Panther leaders suggested that black policemen resident in the West Oakland ghetto patrol that ghetto, Gain told the press that the Black Panther Party had "no practical program to offer the police." Black Panther Chairman Bobby Seale suggested that police wouldn't be inclined to do too much brutalizing in the black community if they had to come back and sleep there at night. "Anarchy!" was Mayor Reading's unequivocal reaction, and he added that the idea of his meeting or negotiating with the Black Panther Party was "the most ridiculous suggestion" he had ever heard.

This is the climate in which Huey P. Newton, twenty-six-year-old co-founder (with Bobby Seale) and Defense Minister of the Black Panther Party, was on trial for his life in the Alameda County Courthouse. Newton was charged with the fatal shooting of an Oakland patrolman, John Frey, in a pre-dawn gun battle on October 28, 1967, with the wounding of a second officer, Herbert Heanes, and the kidnaping of a motorist who drove Newton to the hospital. Newton, who pleaded innocent to the charges, was himself shot in the abdomen during the melee. Tension in and around the Alameda County Courthouse was so high that, by order of the presiding judge in the case, seventy-two-year-old Monroe Friedman, even members of the press were frisked before they were permitted to enter the courtroom on the seventh floor. Since the opening day of the trial—July 15, 1968—an array of sheriff's deputies, silver-helmeted and with revolvers and handcuffs at their belts, was stationed inside both the Twelfth Street and Thirteenth Street entrances of this building to which the general public usually has free access. All other doorways were barred. From the sixth floor to the tenth, the stairway was sealed off. On the tenth floor, Huey Newton and other prisoners were held in maximum security.

During the entire day, anyone seeking to enter the courthouse had to be cleared by the sheriff's armed deputies who stood inside the glass doors, stony-jawed, with helmet straps clamped rigidly under their chins. Irritation, anger, and outrage were the prevalent reactions to the massive display of armed security, and there was a good deal of all of these emotions in the voice and eye of the brilliant, hard-hitting defense attorney, Charles Garry, when, on the opening day, he called Judge Friedman's attention to the fact that the sensational security measures being taken were creating an "atmosphere of fear and intimidation" prejudicial to Newton's case. "Every time I enter this court, I feel I am in a police state," Garry said, and Judge Friedman tartly admonished him to confine himself to the issues and not interject "personal matters."

Judge Friedman's own "personal matters," incidentally, present an interesting area for speculation. Engraved in the deep lines of his bleak-eyed, furrowed mask is all the embitterment of having, in 1952, been appointed by then President Truman to a Federal judgeship, and serving almost a year in that capacity, only to have the appointment dropped by President Eisenhower. Friedman, with perhaps the most important racial trial in the history of our country tried under his jurisdiction, is a member of the Oakland Elks Club whose by-laws limit the membership to "white males." Until just a few years ago, this restriction was applied in practice to exclude Jews (as well as blacks) from membership. Because of his prominence as a judge, the ruling against Jews was waived in Friedman's case, and in the ritual swearing-in ceremony, Friedman pledged himself to uphold the by-laws of the club. (As the trial proceeded, Judge Friedman's testiness with the defense attorneys, and his apparent reluctance to overrule the prosecution's objections to defense testimony, made clear where his sympathies lay. This bias was to culminate in his refusal to permit three black defense witnesses to testify that members of the district attorney's office, including Assistant District Attorney Lowell Jensen, had offered to pay, "and pay well," for information about the shooting on October 28th. In ruling against the defense, Friedman pointed out to Garry that "it was not unusual for lawyers to pay for information or"—to put it in a more genteel way—"to pay a witness's expenses.")

From shortly after eight in the morning of July 15th, a gradually amassing crowd of more than two thousand blacks and whites, carrying banners and placards, marched four abreast around the courthouse block. The chanting, shouting, and clamoring of that multitude for their warrior to be set free was accurately described by the *San Francisco Chronicle* as "an awesome outburst."

The only policemen on the streets (at least in uniform) were those directing traffic, while Black Panthers in leather jackets, black trousers, and black berets took their places in designated and disciplined formation against the walls of the courthouse as if, paradoxically enough, guarding it from onslaught. Whenever the crowd showed signs of getting out of control, these uniformed monitors joined hands and formed an encircling barrier.

Only one arrest was made that day, and the man arrested was white. He was twenty-five-year-old Robert B. Avakian, son of Alameda Superior Court Judge Spurgeon Avakian, who tore the American flag from its pole before the courthouse. In its front page story on July 16th, the *Oakland Tribune* stated that "demonstrators pulled down the flag," but it made no mention of the fact that the perpetrator was white, or that he was the son of an Alameda County judge. (If the *Oakland Tribune* owns the district attorney's office, say the skeptical, the reverse is equally true.) The *Oakland Tribune* also failed to note that there were white mothers pushing baby-carriages in that demonstration and that a demonstrating Oakland grandmother was heard to say, "This country had better wake up, or it's in for a hard time."

There was an unmistakable note of jubilation in the tremendous chanting of the marching thousands, and this may well have been because most people there had, until this moment, lived their entire lives as outsiders, without badges or gleaming helmets or press credentials, or even so simple a thing as a job, to give them status. For this one time, they were strong enough in numbers and conviction to be heard, and heard they were, if dimly, as high as the seventh floor courtroom where the articulate, slender, young black man sat at the counsel table with his chief attorney, Garry, and other members of the defense team. Bobby Seale stood on the orange Peace and Freedom Party soundtruck and called for organization, discipline, and "correct tactics," and for a jury of Newton's peers to try him. Newton, he said, is a member of an oppressed society being tried by men and women of a society that has never experienced suppression and never suffered defeat. But the final cry in that all-day supporting action of their leader was: "If anything happens to Huey Newton, the sky's the limit."

Newton himself defines the Black Panther Party as a political party with a political aim. That aim is the liberation of the black people of America through economic revolution, an aim that is inevitably linked with the liberation of the black people of the world. He points out that the black community is in great part unaware of its political plight because black people are largely illiterate or semi-literate, and they are bewildered by the complex solutions politicians express.

The Black Panther Party is seeking to make clear to them, Newton elaborates, that politics and power are a matter of decent housing, food, clothing, and financial security. "We are an activist group," he stated in a recent interview, "and the purpose of that activity is to raise the consciousness of the black community . . . A basic solution would be for black people to declare themselves a separate nation and invite representatives from the United Nations to see that their rights are respected. Blacks could assert the right to secede from a mother country which has always treated them unfairly. However, we are working with white mother country radicals, and we see a definite place for them in the economic revolution . . . Spontaneous riots are not recommended, for discipline and direction are essential to our cause . . ." (Black Panthers look on the black community as a colonized country, occupied and policed by whites. Thus the titles Minister of Defense, Minister of Information, and so on, are governmental rather than political party titles.)

The defense maintained that Newton is a political prisoner, and that he was stopped by the police in the early hours of October 28th because of his political activities. But the talk among the armed and helmeted men in the halls of the Oakland courthouse, and among truck drivers drinking their early morning coffee in Alameda County roadside eating places, was that when all the Panthers have been liquidated, the ghetto will be without its agitators, and law and order will prevail. "Thirty million black people cannot be wiped out," said Huey Newton quietly, "although there is every reason to believe their leaders will be."

There are sixty-two seats in the courtroom in which the Newton trial took place, of which twenty-eight were reserved for the press. Garry, a man with a twenty-year record of fighting for—and winning—criminal cases in which race or class prejudice (or both) played a controlling part, had requested a larger courtroom so that any number of spectators could be accommodated. Friedman rejected this request, but on the first day of the trial he interrupted the testimony on Garry's main motion—that the entire master panel from which jurors were to be selected should be thrown out—to instruct the court bailiffs "to fill the spectators' seats." Friedman announced that he didn't want to see "a single seat vacant in this courtroom," and as he settled back in his chair he seemed quite pleased with this highly democratic gesture he had made. Yet he must have known that it was little short of a miracle for anyone without official business in the courthouse to get past the guns and helmets and handcuffs at the entrance doors below.

This was not the only request which Charles Garry, who looks ten years younger than his fifty-nine years, was to lose in those first days. While he argued for the dismissal of the entire jury panel of eighteen hundred persons, on the grounds that Newton's rights under the Fourteenth Amendment were violated by the biased selection procedure, members of the legal defense team were unsuccessfully attempting to convince the Federal judiciary in San Francisco that Newton's trial should be halted until a full hearing could be held on Newton's 1964 felony conviction. (Newton had not been represented by counsel on the previous occasion.)

However, one request that Garry made July 15th was, surprisingly enough, conceded to. This was that Newton's fiancée, LaVerne Williams, and his minister, the Reverend Earl Neil of St. Augustine's Church, should be permitted to be present in the courtroom at all times during the proceedings. But even this was a short-lived triumph, for at the close of that first day, Garry, tight-lipped and quick on his feet despite a tendency to weight, informed Judge Friedman that his Honor's directive had been overruled by the sheriff's office on the second floor, and that Miss Williams and Father Neil would not be permitted to re-enter the courtroom until they had been fingerprinted and mugged. "Never in my born days," Garry declared, "have I heard of spectators being subjected to this kind of treatment." Friedman, scrawny as a molting eagle, swept his long black robe around him as he rose from his high throne, and snapped: "If you have a motion to file, present it in the regular manner. This court is in recess . . ."

The three opening days of the trial, when Garry and his dedicated legal aides fought vigorously imaginatively (and again unsuccessfully) to have the panel of veniremen dismissed, undoubtedly presented the greatest opportunity for distinguished and pioneer judicial action that has ever come Judge Friedman's way. Here was the flood tide of his career, and had he but recognized that moment, his name might have had a secure and enviable place in California legal history. But one simple question which Friedman asked July 16th of a recognized authority on the jury system, whom Garry had put on the stand, was proof enough that the shabby choice had been made and the brief moment that had been offered Friedman for stature was now past.

"Are you trying to say it is your opinion that a white jury is more likely to convict a Negro?" Friedman asked in a tone of outrage of Dr. Hans Zeisel, Professor of Law at the University of Chicago, and co-author of a respected work, *The American Jury,* who in 1954–55 made a study of what constitutes particular biases in jurors. Dr. Zeisel spread his hands and smiled, and a titter ran through the courtroom as he replied with disarming tact and grace: "It is rumored that it has happened."

Friedman had heard Edward Keating, former publisher of *Ramparts* and a lawyer now assisting the defense, testify that he and other members of the team had spent the entire night studying thousands of Alameda County jury recruitment records. They had found that a higher percentage of prospective jurors from West Oakland (the black ghetto) is systematically excused from jury duty than prospective jurors from Alameda County as a whole.

Judge Friedman had also heard, provided he wished to hear, that some thirty percent of the registered voters of West Oakland (the area from which Huey Newton comes) are disqualified from serving on the jury panel. And he had heard Garry declare that "the voter registration list used is unconstitutional, discriminatory, and unjust." He had heard Dr. Jan Dizard, Assistant Professor of Sociology at the University of California at Berkeley, testify that eighty-two percent of the eligible voters in Alameda County are registered to vote, while in heavily Negro populated West Oakland only 52.5 percent are registered.

"Do you know of any physical or legal barring of their right to register to vote?" Judge Friedman demanded, and Dr. Dizard replied that it was entirely psychological and sociological. "The Negro population views the government as a relatively hostile and foreign apparatus," Dizard said.

"We know of the deprivation, the hunger, and all that typifies the ghetto of West Oakland," Garry said. "To say that they are free to vote is not the answer. They do not acknowledge letters because they are afraid their creditors may catch up with them. They are totally disillusioned with our white racist society, and so they do not register to vote. Huey Newton has the right to the voice of the thirty percent from his community who have not registered."

Judge Friedman had heard Dr. Floyd Hunter, head of the Social Science and Research and Development Corporation in Berkeley, testify that Negroes are less likely to register to vote than whites because of their apathy toward a political system which they feel excludes them. He had just completed a study of social relationships and behavioral programs for the U.S. Department of Commerce, and in the past ten years had made a study of power structures across the United States which resulted in a book entitled *Top Leadership, USA*. But his conclusion that Negroes are, on the whole, so frustrated by their meaningless place in a white society that they are apathetic to civic action, did not provide Judge Friedman with food for thought.

"If there is any physical interference with the registration of voters in Alameda County, whether black, white, yellow, or brown, I want to know about it," Judge Friedman said indignantly, and the impassable barrier between free and enlightened discussion and self-deceiving obliquity now divided the issues and the protagonists even more finally than before.

Lowell Jensen, the prosecutor, became assistant district attorney in Alameda County in 1967. In his early forties, Jensen is tall, quiet-spoken, and so disciplined that every word, gesture, and reflex appear to be kept in hand by an almost alarming self-control. It is not immediately apparent that the straitjacket that restricts him is actually fear.

Three years ago, Jensen told me, an accused murderer awaiting trial in the Alameda County Courthouse, had tried to shoot his way out of the maximum security tenth floor jail with a gun that had been smuggled in to him, and the implication behind this statement was that Huey P. Newton might try to do the same. Before Jensen would be able to grasp the meaning of such sentences as, "It is a basic tenet of the party dogma that a Panther fires only in self-defense," or, "Shooting incidents between the police and the Panthers have invariably been initiated by the police," he would have to learn to read and give ear to an entirely new tongue.

When asked, as I did, if the prosecution process becomes within a brief time a game as impersonal as chess, a series of maneuvers and counter-moves in which compassion and justice finally have no part, Jensen replied that every man in the D. A.'s office is wholly convinced of the rightness of the people's cause before he undertakes to prosecute a case. Is it only the men in the district attorney's office then, it occurs to the naive, who are not required by judicial custom to presume a man innocent until his guilt is proved?

In the course of the jury selection days which lay ahead, Jensen challenged all those prospective jurors who were unalterably opposed to capital punishment, in the ruthless hope of filling the twelve seats with men and women who would not be averse to recommending the gas chamber for the accused.

So there was Jensen, an almost catatonic figure, functioning as death's advocate in the courtroom, and there were Garry's experts, a quite different breed of men. They had long since evolved from the acceptance of one-dimensional concepts of good and evil, and their informed concerns were the multiple nuances which constitute light and shadow in the landscape of any man's identity. Dr. Zeisel and Dr. Nevitt Sanford, Professor of Psychology at Stanford University, and Director of the university's Institute for the Study of Human Problems, were among the seven authorities Garry put on the stand in the three days that he argued the motion to dismiss the jury panel. The testimony they gave opened an area of conjecture so wide and unencumbered that, as they spoke, the courtroom seemed even smaller and more inadequate than it had before. Death was put in its proper place and assigned its exact percentage, but neither Friedman nor Jensen seemed able—or willing—to weigh the value of what was being said.

Among the eleven hundred jurors Dr. Zeisel had interviewed in preparing his book, *The American Jury*, he found that fifty-five percent of white men polled approved of capital punishment, while not more than thirty-five percent of black men did. In the case of women, forty-two percent white were in favor of capital punishment compared to thirty-one percent of black. He testified that those jurors he had questioned who favored capital punishment were twenty-eighty percent for open housing, while those opposed to the death penalty were fifty-nine percent for open housing. He spoke with wit, authority, and a quickness of eye and gesture that suggested alert thinking was the most stimulating exercise conceivable, as he provided figures, not adjectives, to describe the enemy's hideously inhuman face.

"Being for or against capital punishment divides people into two very different categories," Dr. Zeisel said. "Those who are pro-capital punishment are likely to side with the prosecution in a case rather than with the defendant." And he added that men may vary their responses slightly on relatively unimportant matters, but on matters of moment, such as approval or disapproval of war, or the question of life or death, men's answers tend to remain constant.

Dr. Sanford, one of the first of the University of California in Berkeley professors to refuse to sign the loyalty oath more than a decade ago, is a silvery-haired, tall, slender man of exceptional distinction. He testified that in preparation of his book *The Authoritarian Personality,* fifteen hundred persons had been interviewed over a period of six years, using what he termed the "F-Scale" to classify certain personality traits. His study had been begun in the last year of World War II, and the F-Scale had been conceived as an instrument for measuring anti-Semitism, the "F" standing then, as now, for Fascist. At the top of the F-Scale are those who are over-submissive to authority, who adhere rigidly to conventional values, and who have a tendency to be aggressive toward those who defy—or even appear to defy—authoritative values. Prejudice concerning class or race, Sanford said, is very much a part of the authoritarian personality, and people with such prejudice are inclined to be suspicious, punitive, and ready to believe the worst about human nature. In his cross-examination of Sanford, Jensen put to him what might be classified as a suspicious question. "What term or terminology did you come up with for those low on the F-Scale?" he asked, and Sanford replied: "Antiauthoritarian or low authoritarian, such as religious people, genuine liberals, or the type of person who is against all authority." Judge Friedman leaned forward and asked rather caustically if Sanford had any statistics on the number of high F-Scale persons in Alameda County.

Jensen put only one witness on the stand during this phase of the trial, a respectable, middle-aged, rather nervously complacent lady who had been a jury clerk for thirteen years. In testifying that the selection of names for the jury panel had always been made from the voter registration lists and had worked out very satisfactorily, she appeared to take her place at the top of the F-Scale where authority is beyond question or reproach. And here Garry cried out that if the prosecution's argument were sustained there would be no progress in history.

"I intend to attack the system of jury panel selection in municipal court as I have in this Superior Court," Garry shouted. "It is only because lawyers have questioned established procedure that progress has been made."

On July 17th, however, Judge Friedman denied without comment Garry's motion to have the jury panel dismissed. On Garry's second motion (that prospective jurors not be excluded for cause if they were opposed to capital punishment), Friedman said he would be guided by the recent U. S. Supreme Court decision in the Witherspoon case. Jensen, in conversation with reporters, interpreted this as leaving him free to excuse for cause prospective jurors who stated they were reluctant to impose the death penalty. Both the prosecution and the defense, under California law, are allowed twenty peremptory challenges for the dismissal of jury candidates without stating a reason for the dismissal, while challenges for cause (of which both sides have an unlimited number) must be ruled on by the court.

On July 17th, Huey Newton, quietly self-assured and eagerly communicative, received the press in a visitor's cell on the tenth floor of the courthouse. In response to questions, Newton said he believed he would get a fair trial if the court respected the law and the Constitution and gave him a jury of his peers. By this, he explained, he did not mean that the jury should be entirely made up of black people, but rather people from and involved in his community, West Oakland. Whites would be entirely acceptable, he said, if they had similar economic status to his and used a similar language. Different languages are spoken between black and black, and white and white, he added, because black people and white come from different countries. The white upper class, for instance, has no understanding of, and does not use the language spoken by, the poor.

On July 18th, forty-seven prospective jurors, of whom five were black, filed into the courtroom, and the selection process began. In the nine days ahead, the questions which Garry put to these men and women are perhaps in essence the questions we should each ask ourselves when we are quite alone with the beating of our own hearts.

"Would you give more credence to a policeman's testimony than to that of another person?" was one of the questions Garry put to the jury candidates. Other questions he asked were:

"Have you ever had a bad experience with a black person?"

"Would you object if black people moved into your neighborhood?"

"Would the fact that the Black Panther Party opposes the war in Vietnam make a difference to you in your judgment of this case?"

"Have you any objection to the term Black Power?"

"If you were Huey Newton and you were on trial for your life, would you feel you were going to get a fair trial if you, as you are now, were in the jury box?"

"Have you any objection to the Black Panther Party seeking to elucidate the grievances of the Negro ghetto?"

The answers to the double question as to whether or not a prospective juror had read the Kerner Report, or ever heard of it, were the most revealing and disheartening of all. While almost without exception every man and woman questioned read the *Oakland Tribune* daily, only three or four out of the nearly two hundred questioned had heard of the Kerner Report (the Report of the National

Advisory Commission on Civil Disorders). None had read it. Thus they were unaware that in this 1967 investigation of the causes of civil disorders in the United States—an investigation ordered by President Johnson—the blue-ribbon Commission had reached a number of deeply disturbing conclusions. Among these were: that our nation is moving toward two societies, one black, one white—separate and unequal; that to pursue our present course in the handling of civil disorders involves the ultimate destruction of basic democratic values; that white racism is essentially responsible for the explosive mixture that has been building in our cities since the end of World War II; that the principal official response to civil disorders has been to equip the police with more sophisticated weapons; that the realization of common opportunities for all within a single society requires of every American new attitudes, new understanding, and, above all, new will.

On July 30th, Garry asked that census tracts be used in addition to registration lists for the selection of the master jury panel, but this too was rejected by the court. And on that same day the twelve regular jurors were sworn in and the process of choosing four alternate jurors began.

The Newton jury (including the alternates) wound up with one Nego (a loan officer in a bank), one man of Japanese ancestry, three persons with Spanish surnames (one of these a native of Cuba), a cosmetic saleswoman, a second banker, a machinist, two housewives, a bologna slicer, an engineer property owner, and three employes of, respectively, a food packing firm, a paper company, and an airline food catering service. Among them was no one who might be classified as being of Newton's peer group.

By August 1st, a panel of 160 jury candidates had been called, setting a record, it was said, for Alameda County Superior Court. Jensen, over Garry's protests, had managed to dismiss every Negro who had been called—twenty-one in all—except for the banker, and Garry accused Jensen of having devised a method—which was with a total lack of impartiality upheld by Friedman—to exclude from the jury any man or woman who stated an unalterable opposition to the death penalty.

But there were two candidate jurors whose voices should be listened to for a moment here. Each of them spoke briefly in the courtroom.

The young woman appeared to be little older than a school girl, dark-haired, with the kind of beauty that requires no make-up. Despite her apparent nervousness, she spoke out clearly, saying she could not be an impartial juror because she was prejudiced by the circumstances. She was very much aware, she said, of the conflicts taking place in our country, and she believed it was not one man's guilt or innocence, but white racism, that was the real factor in this case.

The other voice was that of a lean, stoop-shouldered, olive-skinned man with thinning black hair and work-worn hands, and it spoke in the tough, aggressive accents of one who had lived a long time in a lower class, discriminatory hell, and who was not going to take any more from anyone at all. He was from Hawaii, he said, where dark-skinned people are treated like human beings, and he had never seen anything like what went on here.

"I have a Chinese-Hawaiian son, darker than me," he said, "and he's blamed for all kinds of violence he didn't do. He's maybe sitting home all night watching the TV with me, and they come in to get him for something that happened maybe two blocks away. My best friends, he's a black man married to a white lady, they had to move out of the neighborhood where they lived. I know how blacks are treated in California. Nobody can tell me anything about that. I've never seen nothing like it anywhere."

Both of these prospective jurors were challenged for cause by Jensen, over Garry's spirited protests, and Judge Friedman upheld the prosecution's challenges, wrapped the black robes of justice around him, settled back in his chair, and went to sleep again.

No
One
Can
Be
All
Things
to
All
People

IN MAY 1969, I WAS COMMISSIONED BY THE *Chicago Sun-Times* to interview Huey P. Newton, Minister of Defense of the Black Panther Party. Newton (now twenty-eight years old) was convicted of voluntary manslaughter in Oakland, California, in September 1968 for the death of an Oakland policeman, John Frey. Newton is now serving a two- to fifteen-year term in the Mens Colony near San Luis Obispo. For twelve months I have been in correspondence with the Department of Corrections in Sacramento, and with Superintendent Harold V. Field of the Mens Colony, in an attempt to get permission for an interview. I do not know what the civil rights of prisoners are. Perhaps they have none. But I do know that though Huey Newton's chief attorney, Charles Garry, approves of my seeing his client, and even though Newton himself would like to see me (and even though I have been asked by a daily newspaper to interview Newton), the prison authorities of California will not grant me the permission to do so.

A year ago Superintendent Field wrote to me that "due to the continued rejection of the correctional program by Newton, his refusal to accept any assignment, and his present attitude which appears to be more rejecting after interviews of the type you request, we are not permitting same." (I was, of course, not requesting any particular "type" of interview.) Less than two weeks after Mr. Field's first letter to me, an information officer in the Department of Corrections rejected with quite a different explanation my appeal for the reversal of Mr. Field's decision. The information officer wrote in part:

> Shortly after Mr. Newton arrived at California Mens Colony, it became evident, due to the large number of interview requests, that we could not follow the usual procedure. We were reluctant to prohibit all interviews. Thus, it was decided to permit interviews only by full-time staff reporters for general coverage daily newspapers or for daily general news programs on radio or television. We have adhered very strictly to this policy. Many writers, some of considerable stature, have sought interviews and have been turned down.

The most recent letter I received from Superintendent Field is dated February 20, 1970. In it he advised me that "our policy has not changed." But this policy is interpreted one way in Los Padres, where the California Mens Colony is situated, and another way in Sacramento, and one can only fi-

nally conclude that the reason for this stringent ruling is due to quite other considerations. It may well
be that the restricting of interviews with Huey Newton, who is now an internationally-known figure, is
to keep writers who might respect his political
convictions from direct contact with him, and also
to prevent the black press from speaking with an
idolized leader whose image has acquired the di-
mensions of myth. There are few black daily news-
papers around, and even fewer that deal in "general
coverage." But reports on Huey Newton are not
lacking. One of his attorneys told me recently that
he is now as completely contained within the
stronghold of his dedication as was Gandhi. On
May 11th of this year, a friend of mine (who ful-
filled the stipulated requirements for interviewing
Huey Newton) told me that his eyes were "bright,
alert, warm. A soft look. Not unlike that of Cesar
Chavez. Like a person who has overcome his fear of
death." And this same friend (George Williams of
The Sacramento Bee) added: "I cannot emphasize
enough how fresh he appeared, mentally, physically, spiritually—as if he were a monk just emerg-
ing from years of meditation in a mountain-top
monastery."

I have not been permitted to interview Huey
Newton, but I have at least been able to study at
some length the booklet issued by the Mens Colony,
presumably under the editorship of Mr. Field. This
booklet reads in part like a brochure describing a
retirement home for the genteel aged. In his introduction, Mr. Field points out that the photo-

graphs in the pamphlet "depict people learning, doing, and living." These photographs show us, for instance, "elderly inmates [participating] in a varied recreational program," and the caption of one particularly sun-drenched scene reads: "Shuffleboard is one of the more popular sports enjoyed by this group." Another photograph is captioned: "In the spring, the crack of a bat against the horsehide signifies that the national pastime is underway." There is no photograph in which weapons of any kind are in evidence, and only one showing actual prison bars.

Shuffleboard and baseball, tennis, handball, boxing, a knitting mill, a shoemaking shop, a tobacco factory, a textile products factory, a sheet metal shop—all these are reassuringly depicted and described. No mention is made of religious services, or of library facilities, but perhaps one should not jump too quickly to the conclusion that there are no weapons, no religious services, and few iron bars in the California Mens Colony. After all, it is stated in the booklet that academic training is provided, and that "approximately forty-five percent of the Mens Colony inmates participate in the educational program." This would seem a rather low percentage for a prison population of 2,380, composed for the most part (we are told) of men of "normal intelligence."

According to the brochure, the sojourners at this Colony receive "excellent medical and dental care," and they are free to join a landscape gardening class, or "a nationally affiliated speech club," or a "puppeteers' club," or a drama club. They may also attend regular "sing outs," edit publications, or collect postage stamps. Another photograph in this handsome booklet shows rows of beds on either side of a gleaming middle aisle, and the caption advises us that "a restful atmosphere prevails" in the prison's hospital wards. Indeed, the California Mens Colony would seem a far better place for a man to live his life in than a city ghetto or on an Indian reservation. Moreover, judging from the photographs, there appear to be fewer cops around than on the campus of San Francisco State College.

"No one can be all things to all people," states the pamphlet; but it hastens to add that "the Correctional Officer comes close." The Correctional Officer would seem to be all that they, the inmates of this colony, had needed all their lives, and who has now made a belated appearance on their scene. We learn that the Correctional Officer counsels and advises the sojourner here on "how to get along with his peers in a free society, why various types of behavior are not approved or condoned in the institution or in society, and by means of regularly scheduled counts make certain that the inmates remain within the confines of the institution." (My friend, George Williams, tells me there is a double barbed-wire fence, with twelve feet of space between each section, and eight watchtowers placed at regular intervals along the fence, so there would seem to be little opportunity for an inmate to get outside the "confines of the institution.")

The pamphlet makes clear that the Correctional

Officer comes close to being all things to all people because of his friendly counselling, and because he even becomes at times a trusted "confidante." (That's the feminine form of the word, Mr. Field. You should have checked on that.) The Correctional Officer, says the text, "helps each man to re-focus his aims, his perception of self." But as one reads one asks oneself about the aims and the self of political prisoners such as Huey Newton. Would not the Correctional Officer's "counsel" be more in the nature of a condemnation of the value of the political prisoner's beliefs? Huey Newton keeps himself apart because he knows that prison must, of necessity, destroy individual conviction. The individual, whatever his name, whatever his crime, must be fragmented, and then the pieces of the man and his beliefs can be reassembled in a quite different mold. This is rehabilitation. This is the way of saving not the "perception of self" but the correctional system's perception of our society.

Huey Newton has not been rehabilitated. He has kept himself intact. "In my nineteen months here," he said on May 11, 1970, in the interview I did not have with him, "I have spent twenty-one hours of each day locked up in my cell. I am released for meals . . . I have some free time after eating. How long depends on how long I have to stand in line before eating. On my way back to my cell, I exercise in the yard by walking around or by working out on the high bar and parallel bars. I chin myself or do some exercises I've worked out for myself on the bars. I use dynamic tension, something I've been doing for years . . . tensing my muscles, then relaxing them, then tensing them. This accounts for all my free time—under an hour each day. They allow me to do this begrudgingly."

Begrudgingly, because Huey Newton has refused to work. Five hundred out of the present inmate population are employed in the prison industries, and this, too, seems an astonishingly small percentage, but this is the figure the pamphlet provides. "I will not be treated as a slave," Newton states, "regardless of the consequences . . . What we have to do is organize some dynamic form of passive resistance. The prisoners must be made to understand that the institution couldn't exist one day without the labor of the inmates . . . There are only one or two staff cooks, for example; the rest are prisoners. The same is true of the factories and offices." Those who work an eight-hour day in the various "programs" of the prison start at three cents an hour and may eventually reach the maximum wage of ten cents an hour. "They could demand union wages and better working conditions," Newton suggests, "and then we could even negotiate to pay our room and board."

In Newton's words, the consequences of his refusal to "program" are: "I am not allowed library privileges. They removed the earphones from my room . . . this is a radio broadcast hookup, just one station. I am allowed ten books in my room at any one time. But I must order them from the publisher, and they must be approved by the superintendent. And they must relate to my appeal." He sat there in the Attorneys' Room, wearing a light blue denim shirt, and darker trousers which were heavily starched, giving him a sharp, almost military appearance. Other prisoners had refused to "program," he told George Williams, but they had all been quickly transferred out. "The longest anyone has been locked up the way I am is two weeks," he said; and then he spoke of the prisoners who had associated with him, that is, who had sat with him during meals or passed notes to him. Some were black and some were white, he said, but all of them (approximately ten) were sent to other prisons because of their interest in him. "There was one man, Kenny Favre," he said, "a model prisoner, enrolled in college correspondence courses, an excellent record. The superintendent called him in and told him to stop associating with me. Favre told him he would obey regulations but that no one could tell him who he was to associate with. Favre was transferred to San Quentin." (In a recent telephone conversation, a spokesman for the Mens Colony prison denied that any inmates had been transferred out because of their association with Huey Newton. "It is true that some of the men who have been transferred have associated with Huey Newton," this spokesman said. "But this is only a coincidence. Their association with him was in no way a reason for their transfer." However, the Adult Authority records at San Quentin show that Favre was transferred from the Mens Colony precisely because of his association with Newton.)

The Colony is divided into two separate enclaves, one designated as the East Facility, the other as the West Facility. The West Facility is officially described as "a minimum security institution"; the East as "a medium security institution." Newton is confined in the latter facility. He said that most of his fellow inmates are rejects from other prisons, either social rejects for various reasons, or men with definite mental disorders, or homosexuals. Those who are mentally disturbed are confined in one of the four quadrangles of six hundred cells which make up the facility. (These particular cases had not been mentioned in the brochure, nor were the eighty percent whom Newton says are homosexual.) "They are sensitive to the threat of being shipped out to other prisons," Newton said of the latter, "so they stay in line. There is always the fear that they will be separated from their partners. The authorities would like the public to believe the men are isolated in their separate rooms, but each prisoner has a key, and they can let themselves in and out of one another's rooms." Newton, too, has his own key, but after he locks his cell door, the guard double locks it with another key. (A prison spokesman divulged recently that Timothy Leary is now in the Mens Colony, and appears willing to be "programmed.")

Newton sat talking in a warm and friendly way on May 11th of this year, with no sign of bitterness or depression discernible, speaking about the party he and Bobby Seale had founded together, and whose tenets now constitute a major share of his strength.

"The press generally is very misinformed about the philosophy of the Black Panther Party," he said. "The press either ignores that philosophy or writes of it inaccurately. For example, this anti-white thing. The press assumes that the party is anti-white. This is, of course, untrue. The party really believes in the principles of humanism with regard to people, and socialism with regard to the structure of government and society. The problems of capitalism cannot be solved by capitalistic methods. There must be some form of collectivism which has a primary interest to serve the people—all the people—not one ethnic group. People must have final control over the administration of their government. This must be based on proportional representation within an ethnic framework. It is the only realistic way because of the ethnic pluralism of our country.

"Justice Douglas explained it well in his recent book," Huey Newton went on. "The public sector must be expanded. That is, the group which is served by the government must be broadened to include all of the people, not just the small percentage which is now representative of the ruling class. Agencies must be publicly owned—railroads, oil refineries, farms—instead of the present system in which special interests representing these sectors subvert the public sector for their own good. For example, Senator Eastland gets large subsidies for *not* growing on his Mississippi farmland. This is welfare. Yet . . . he is not under constant harassment, nor is he persecuted, as are millions of poor people on welfare."

On that particular day when, for just over an hour, he was able to make his views known to the media, Huey Newton said that "any talk of a wide-spread racial war in this country or armed revolution is strictly romanticism. Blacks cannot do it alone. They must work in coalition with whites who are politically awakened. But they must retain strict control of their own parties. The Black Panther Party must be controlled by blacks. Blacks can awaken other blacks. They cannot awaken whites, but they can involve whites in the correct political perspective and help them to awaken other whites . . . This system we hope to achieve—this socialist system with proportional representation—won't necessarily wipe out racism . . . It will take a long time . . . In the meantime, while the changes are being made, there must be self-defense. The Black Panther Party has this responsibility—to provide defense for the black community while there is still racism."

The deputy superintendent who spoke with George Williams after the interview with Huey Newton was done said that he respected Newton.

"Huey maintains he is a political prisoner and should not be made to work," the deputy superintendent said. "But he was sent to us as a convicted felon and will be treated as any other. He also says he will not work for slave wages. He wants us to pay the minimum wage of $1.65 an hour. I would be glad to do this, but the legislature sets the wage scale in the prisons. We are stuck with it. Huey is a man of strong convictions, and he sticks to his convictions. More power to him for that."

In the total silence of this interview which was not granted me, I told Huey Newton that the voice of prison authority was decking out with fancy statements its inability to deal with Man. "No one can be all things to all people," it was saying with the wiliest of smiles.

On May 29, 1970, the Court of Appeal in San Francisco reversed Huey Newton's conviction. The court held that the trial court in Oakland had committed prejudicial error in not instructing the jury to acquit if it found that Newton was unconscious at the time Police Officer Frey was shot. Both Huey Newton and Dr. Bernard Diamond, University of California Professor of Law and Criminology, had so testified at the Oakland trial. The appellate court in San Francisco also found it erroneous not to have given Newton a hearing on his claim that a felony conviction several years earlier was unconstitutional and invalid inasmuch as he was not represented by counsel at the time.

The appellate court further cited as erroneous that the Oakland court had not reopened the trial when the defense discovered that the only eyewitness to the shooting of Frey had said, an hour and a half after the incident, that he had *not* seen the assailant's face. (At the trial, this same witness had testified that the assailant was Newton.)

The appellate court's decision will be final sixty days from May 29th. Unless discharged completely, Newton could be retried only on manslaughter, the charge on which he was convicted, and manslaughter is a bailable offense. The State has the right to appeal the reversal of Newton's conviction to the California Supreme Court; but at this writing, the highest court to rule on the case has determined the conviction to be invalid. If Huey's skin were white, there is every reason to believe that he would at this moment be free on bail.

Seeing
the
Sights
in
San Francisco

THERE ARE ANY NUMBER OF VERY UNIQUE SPOTS OF interest in this vicinity which are, unfortunately, not known to the majority of tourists who flock throughout the year to our beautiful and festive city. I have jotted down a few notes about two or three of these off-the-beaten-track places which vacationers should not fail to see.

Last year I frequently suggested to sojourners in these parts that Sunday was the best day of the week to make a tour of the fabulous Golden Gate Cemetery which lies in all its verdant beauty in the rolling countryside just beyond South San Francisco. On Sunday, one did not at that time run the weekday risk of being delayed an hour or more at the gates by half a dozen or so hearses bearing flag-draped coffins, and by the unavoidable accompanying press of the cars of families and friends.

Happily, this year the same problem does not exist on any day of the week, for practically every well-tended inch of that vast, flowering expanse is now symmetrically covered with gleaming white headstones. As of late June, only the dependents of servicemen already resting there are being accepted, and this makes for a far more leisurely atmosphere. Thus a visit may be planned for any day that suits the sight-seer's schedule. On one side, under the bluest of California skies, he will see the sparkling waters of the Pacific, and on the other, beyond the flowering area, he will see, rising in dramatic contrast, the wild, barren hills which the government hopes soon to be able to procure for further cultivation.

Once having reached this scenic wonderland, it will be well worth your while to leave your car or bus on arrival and stroll down the spacious, well-kept avenues that wind around and almost seem to embrace the grassy slopes. Thanks to the noted clemency of our winters, an endless profusion of gladioli, iris, roses in a variety of colors, and gold and white chrysanthemums, presents a year-round breathtaking horticultural display.

Indeed, the abundance of flowers often makes it difficult to find the temporary markers which supply the names of those who lie under these freshly spread coverlets. But if you take a moment to kneel down and push aside some of the floral offerings you may read on neatly typed cards, framed in metal and covered with sturdy transparent plastic, that Pfc. Stuart Hawkins, for instance, of the U.S. Infantry died on May 20, 1967, and was laid to rest here on May 26, 1967; or that Lt. David O'Hara of the U.S. Marines died on June 18, 1967, and was interred in this beautiful spot on June 23rd. It may cross your mind before you get up from your knees that just six weeks or so ago Private First Class Hawkins and Lieutenant O'Hara were walking around the streets of Saigon or Danang or somewhere like that, and this is quite an arresting thought. Indeed, after visiting this and other out-of-the-way sites, you will have an endless stream of unusual memories to take home with you.

Background to this particular off-beat outing is readily available to tourists who can spare the time for a brief visit to the mortuary home on Valencia, situated in the famous Mission District of the city. One of the interesting sights there is the arrival of Navy trucks from Travis Air Force Base several times a day. Each truck is equipped with tiers of shelves, or berths resembling those of a sleeping car, on which have been placed long aluminum containers, conveniently numbered and tagged. On each container, stencilled in black, are the words, DO NOT TIP. This is because the contents have been packed in ice at the Tan Son Nhut Air Base in Saigon, and, despite the high degree of refrigeration, there may be some loose water in the container by the time it reaches its destination. The Travis Mortuary Affairs office, however, is justifiably proud of the fact that never during the course of any previous war have erstwhile combatants been transported within such a short lapse of time from the battlefield to the embalmer's table.

It is not at all unusual for the remains of returning servicemen to reach the base three or four days after demise in Vietnam.

Travis Air Force Base itself should not be overlooked as a site of truly exceptional interest. It has the distinction of being the one base to receive *all* the containers flown in from Southeast Asia. They travel on C-141-A jets, poetically known as Starlifters, and these giant military birds, carrying a mixed cargo, touch down on the runway at the rate of thirty or forty every twenty-four hours. The containers, speedily emptied of their contents at the Valencia funeral parlor, are then returned by truck to Travis, loaded on to Starlifters, and rushed back to Tan Son Nhut Air Base to serve again. Some of them—and this is reassuring confirmation of the rigid economy practiced by our military—have been in use since the Korean War.

Another example of the forethought with which this operation is handled may be noted in the fact that, the embalming completed, a one-man military escort accompanies each individual flag-draped coffin to its home destination. That destination may be as far from San Francisco as New Jersey or Rhode Island, or as close as Nevada or Washington State, but there is no doubt in the minds of the military authorities, or in that of the director of the funeral home, that wherever the young man's family may reside, this official gesture is highly valued. The military escort usually spends the night in the former serviceman's home, and it is customary for a brief notice to this effect to appear in the social

144

column of the local paper. "It's a kind of status thing, and the family appreciates it very much," the director of the Valencia funeral parlor told me.

It is also fascinating to watch the sleek Navy limousines making their daily deliveries to this efficiently-run funeral home. Each limousine, fitted with clothes-racks, brings as many as twelve or fifteen fine new uniforms to the mortuary. Dark blue and trimmed in scarlet and gold, they are carried with scrupulous care into the tastefully decorated interior of the funeral parlor. On one of my visits there, I learned that there is frequently not enough left of the young serviceman himself to fit into the uniform the Army provides. The director, a personable young man with three young children and an attractive wife who live right there in the funeral home with him, was kind enough to invite me in to view some of the remains so that I might understand the problems with which he is faced. "It is far from being an enjoyable business," he confided.

If the interested visitor wishes to explore even further behind the scenes, he will learn that competitive bidding in the San Francisco funeral services world has been brisk. But the director of the particular home on Valencia, who got the government contract in 1966, maintains that it is not as profitable a deal as the number of bodies processed every week might lead one to believe. "By the time they are ready to go home, they all look just as life-like as the art we practice can make them," one of the embalming assistants told me. "We give the same care and attention to the preparation of servicemen as we would if they were on a retail basis. We feel we owe it to the boy's family that he goes home looking just as good as he did when he went away—and sometimes even better."

For a complete change of scene, I would suggest a day at Port Chicago on the other side of the bay. This sleepy little town is a pleasant hour-and-a-half drive from downtown San Francisco, and natives claim that it enjoys the best climate in the whole of Northern California. So as to take advantage of every moment of sunlit air and lively sea-breezes, it is recommended that you take a box lunch with you. The seasoned traveler will not feel self-conscious about eating it quite openly, even though a number of hardy visitors who stand before the Naval Weapons Station may be observing a twenty-four-hour fast. Few signs are displayed by this handful of young people, and their presence can be easily overlooked. If questioned, they will be glad to tell you that nine percent of all the explosives sent to Vietnam, including napalm bombs, leave from this busy port.

The Naval Station is a leisurely ten-minute walk from the town of Port Chicago, and you will not, of course, be permitted to enter the confines of the station, which is designated as government property, but the distant masts and rigging of the docked munition ships silhouetted against the clear blue sky is the most picturesque of sights.

If taking your lunch with you presents a problem, a simple regional meal may be procured at modest cost in the little restaurant in the heart of town. Lunching there also offers the attraction of first-hand contact and conversation not only with long-time residents of Port Chicago, but also with merchant seamen off cargo ships that have just returned from Vietnam. Enter into the free and easy atmosphere that prevails, and you will come away with a wealth of interesting information. For instance, the property owners of the town are wholly absorbed in a united effort to frustrate the Navy's plans to buy out the town so as to take over the entire area for increased shipping facilities. As one store owner put it to me, "I don't care what happens in Vietnam, but I'm not going to sell my four lots to the Navy for $700 each when each one of them is worth $1,200." Another resident said he had no intention of selling his $30,000 home for $11,000, which is what the Navy is offering.

The seamen, speaking in their quaint dialects (many come from the Deep South), will tell you of the difficulties that are encountered in getting crews together. Despite the high pay and the generous bonuses, it is not an easy matter to man the munition freighters. But now and then a note of true jubilation is sounded by those seamen who have amassed small fortunes in war-zone pay. They will now be able to purchase homes for their families, and even finance a son's or daughter's college education. For untrained, unskilled men, such rewards were merely pipe-dreams before. So even war has its unexpected compensations. On one occasion a totally illiterate seaman regaled me with a hilarious story of his attempts, on the trip he had just returned from, to get transportation from Saigon to Danang, through enemy lines, to see his GI son who was in an Army hospital there.

Among the many unusual vistors you will see standing before the gates of the Naval Weapons Station, the most impressive is a blond young man of proud and distinctive bearing who is known to one and all as "Larry." Because he was seen standing there for over a year now, Larry Cooper has become a familiar landmark. The town sheriff, quite a personable young man himself, will stop his official car beside Larry and smile as he greets him, and Larry will lean in through the car window and have a pleasant five-minute chat with this officer of the law. Although Larry's hair is longish, it is neatly trimmed, and although he does have a bright blond Van Dyke beard, he is in no sense a hippie. Indeed, his dignified figure suggests that of an old-time, frontier preacher who has strayed for a moment from the Hollywood set where a Western is being filmed.

Larry describes himself, as "a non-Christian minister of truth," and he says that his hope is to be "a point of light and truth for others to see the dignity of Man." It would be easy to picture him in his dark suit and white shirt, a soft-brimmed hat on his blond head, stepping out of an ambushed stagecoach in the wild and woolly days of the old West and persuading the shame-faced stick-up men to lower their guns and let the stage continue on its way.

148

Other young people standing there before the gates, through which passes a constant stream of armored trucks marked EXPLOSIVES, will tell you Larry is a graduate of a California ministerial school, and indeed there is a suggestion of benediction in the friendly hand he raises in greeting to all who pass. Larry will tell you that it was a merchant seaman he ran into in San Francisco in the spring of 1966 who told him about the shipments from Port Chicago. (The man had made two or three trips to Vietnam and his conscience was beginning to bother him.) And everyone, including the sheriff, knows that Larry stopped a running napalm truck last summer, by standing before it, and that he still has a weekend or two to serve in jail to complete his fifteen-day sentence.

Everyone also knows that Larry has to come out from San Francisco by bus now, as in August of this year the two cars he used to bring visitors over for a day's outing were, one after another, destroyed by fire. The names of the young men from Port Chicago who destroyed the cars are known to Larry, and he raises his hand in greeting to them as well when they roar past in their jalopies, their spit often striking his face or the faces of other visitors standing before this vast expanse of government property.

Before setting out at the end of the day on the beautiful return drive to San Francisco, take a moment or two to pick up a memento from the debris of bright, discarded cans, flowering cactus, and broken bottles that have been tossed by passing motorists. You will find bits and pieces of the shattered frames of what were placards in their time, charred syllables of words which once spelled "women" or "children" or "Vietnam." On my first visit to Port Chicago I had the good luck to find five words intact on a cardboard placard otherwise nearly entirely destroyed by fire. They said, MEN ARE NOT OUR ENEMIES . . . The partially burned and scattered lexicon you can salvage there will always make a fascinating conversation piece, and may even prove one day a unique supplementary document to our current history.

If you feel so disposed before you go, do help Larry pick up the Pepsi-Cola and lemon-pop bottles that didn't break when they were thrown. He turns them in at the Port Chicago grocery store, and the refunded deposit money goes toward paying his bus fare back to town. "For the most part everyone's been very helpful," he will tell you. "Marines as well as the workers who load the ships came out and expressed their sympathy about the destruction of the cars. The men working here and the Navy personnel know we aren't going to be frightened off, and they respect that. They know now that whatever happens, we're here to stay."